30-DAY CHURCH
CHALLENGE

OUTREACH

COMMUNITY

WORSHIP

STEWARDSHIP

GROWTH

WRITTEN BY
BOB HOSTETLER

DISCOVER HOW YOU CAN REACH
YOUR **GOD-GIVEN POTENTIAL**

Published by Outreach, Inc. Vista, CA 92081
www.outreach.com

ISBN: 978-1-935541-69-1

Written by: Bob Hostetler
Weekly Challenge page by: Dr. Hal Seed
Cover Design: Tim Downs
Interior Design: Tim Downs
Edited by: Snapdragon Editorial Group, Tulsa, OK

Printed in the United States of America

The following is a sampling of the things you will discover and begin (or continue) to practice on your journey through these daily readings and challenges:

- Living in community opens the door to growth—and joy—in a way that nothing else does.
- With our redemption comes the call to live differently, to be better.
- In God's eyes, it is "not good" if we are not linked to others in healthy, helpful community.
- Our worship should be a day-by-day and moment-by-moment habit.
- The loving sacrifice of Jesus redeems our fallen souls, restores our fellowship with God, reverses our self-centeredness, and returns us to the purpose for which we were created.
- Worshiping God is like a symphony that begins with praise.
- An ungrateful heart cannot truly worship, because a worshipful life is a grateful life.
- Joy is both the content and the overflow of a worshiping heart.
- Our tendency as human beings is to turn romance into routine, and rhythm into meaningless repetition.
- God cannot give more to those whose hands are already full.
- Prayer will change the person who prays.
- One small step can result in amazing growth and development in a person's life.
- We human beings tend to mistake our role, thinking we are owners when God has repeatedly made it clear that we are not.
- Money is a test. Always.
- Your spending today has a direct correlation to where your heart will be tomorrow.
- Everyone you know is a faithful tither.
- God can take whatever you put in His hands and multiply it.
- Jesus calls us to seek relationships with people not for what we can *get* but for what we can *give*.
- The gospel of Jesus Christ is a "Come and See" gospel.
- Real give-and-take relationships with the people around us will open many doors.
- Jesus did not give up on the people everyone else gave up on—and neither should you.

Finally, this book will have the greatest and longest-lasting impact if you read and use it (see next section, How to Use Your *30-Day Church Challenge* Book) at the same time your church and small-group are participating in the campaign. God bless you for taking this extraordinary challenge!

Accepting the Challenge

How to Use the
30-Day Church Challenge Book

They devoted themselves to the apostles' teaching and to fellowship, to the breaking of bread and to prayer. Everyone was filled with awe at the many wonders and signs performed by the apostles. All the believers were together and had everything in common. They sold property and possessions to give to anyone who had need. Every day they continued to meet together in the temple courts. They broke bread in their homes and ate together with glad and sincere hearts, praising God and enjoying the favor of all the people. And the Lord added to their number daily those who were being saved.
—Acts 2:42–47

Those first followers of Jesus in Jerusalem had an amazing impact on the world. Though the church started with just a handful of people praying in an upper room, they witnessed many signs and wonders. Not one of them was in need, for they shared generously with each other. They prayed and worshiped and ate together daily. And they quickly experienced exponential growth, adding as many as three thousand new members in one day.

Wow! Wouldn't it be great to be part of a church like that? Of course, they had advantages. Some of them had walked with Jesus. They had preachers like Peter, James, and John, and they were in on the ground floor of this new thing called the Church.

Still, they had jobs. And families. And problems. Even persecution. In fact, if you read much further in the book of Acts in the Bible, you may see that the main difference between their church and yours was not in their circumstances. It was in their practices. They "devoted themselves" to things we are not much devoted to. But that can change. And when that changes, we will change. Our churches. Our families. Our lives.

Getting Started in the
30-Day Church Challenge Book

The readings in this *30-Day Church Challenge* book begin on Monday (day one), the day after the official Sunday launch of the campaign. Six daily readings are provided for each week—Monday through Saturday. There are no Sunday readings.

To get the most from this experience, set aside a specific time each day to work on the reading and simple step. This should take no more than twenty minutes, depending of course, on the rate at which you read and the degree to which you apply yourself. Take your time; don't read ahead or try to complete more than one day's reading at a time. They are designed to build on each other, and will have the maximum effect if they are read once a day, ideally, in the morning. This allows you to process and meditate on the topic throughout the day. Also, you will draw the most benefit if you try not to skip readings, forcing yourself to have to play "catch up."

Each "day" in the *30-Day Church Challenge* book contains the following content:

Devotional Lesson
Each day's content begins with a short reading. Most of these won't take you more than three or four minutes. They are designed to get you thinking about a particular aspect of the week's topic.

Scriptures
Carefully selected Scriptures follow the daily reading. Some are drawn from the reading, while others are intended to add to the content of the reading. You are encouraged to look these up in your Bible and read them in their broader context.

Prayer
After the daily reading and the Scripture selections, a prayer has been included. We encourage you not only to read this prayer but to actually pray it—out loud even. You may want to add to it or personalize it in some way in response to your personal thoughts and emotions.

Simple Step

Another component of each day is the Simple Step a small but impactful challenge to help you immediately apply the truth or lesson of the day's reading. These action steps are crucial to making the *30-Day Church Challenge* part of your life throughout the thirty days and beyond.

Journal Page

The final section is a journal page with a question or prompt for you to think about and space to write out your thoughts. Take your time with this, as this activity often produces great insight and important breakthroughs for the participant.

Weekly Challenge Page

After Saturday's reading there is a one-page recap of the weekly challenge. This weekly challenge section will touch upon some of the main points of this week's message, and the primary step that you are being challenged to make in your life.

Small-group Study and Discussion Questions

After the Weekly Challenge page there are two pages of small-group study and discussion questions that should be used in your small-group or Sunday-school class. The small-group study and discussion questions in this book are located at the end of each week, however, your small-group may meet earlier in the week. So you may want to review the thoughts, questions, and Scriptures found in this section before your small-group or Sunday-school class starts. And you will want to bring the book with you to that weekly meeting so you can follow along with the progression of thoughts, Scriptures, and questions being discussed.

You are on the verge of a greater growth experience than you ever thought possible. As you apply yourself to the content in this book, may God apply the content in this book to you—for your growth, for your church's growth, and for His glory.

WEEK ONE PURPOSE
COMMUNITY

Main Message Point: All of us need to be part of a small-group within the church, so that we can experience authentic community through the love, support, and encouragement of others.

THIS WEEK'S CHALLENGE
Commit to joining a small-group, class, or ministry so that you can experience real community.

The Unity in Authentic Community

Everyone has a bad day now and then. Even some weeks and months are better than others. But David seemed to be having a bad *life*, surprising since it had all started out so *good*.

Though he was the youngest in his family, the prophet Samuel had singled him out for recognition and anointed him to be the successor to Saul, the first king of Israel. Not long after that, he faced the giant Philistine Goliath in the Valley of Elah and won a startling victory for King Saul and the people of God. Not long after that, he became a musician in Saul's court at the king's personal request.

That's when everything started going downhill.

Because David was being hailed as a hero, Saul became intensely jealous. On more than one occasion, the king became so enraged that he attacked the young man. Saul used his own daughter to lay a trap that was intended to end David's life. Things couldn't have gotten worse—but they did!

David had at least one thing going for him. He and Jonathan, one of King Saul's sons, had developed a strong and close friendship. Jonathan agreed to be David's secret agent. Once he cleverly and conclusively confirmed that his father intended to kill David, he used a pre-arranged signal to warn David to flee for his life. (See 1 Samuel 20.) The two friends shared an emotional goodbye, and David parted from his friend, left his home, and became a fugitive.

The young hero had no protection and no supplies. He sought refuge wherever he could find it—even among Israel's archenemies, the Philistines. Until he came at last to the cave of Adullam, not far from where he had conquered Goliath.

"When his brothers and his father's household heard about it," the Bible says, *"they went down to him there. All those who were in distress or in debt or discontented gathered around him, and he became their leader"* (1 Samuel 22:1–2).

We don't know for sure, but it may have been in the midst of those circumstances—or others like them—that David wrote, *"How good and pleasant it is when God's people live together in unity! It is like precious oil poured on the head, running down on the beard, running down on Aaron's beard, down on the collar of his robe. It is as if the dew of Hermon were falling on Mount Zion. For there the LORD bestows his blessing, even life forevermore"* (Psalm 133:1–3).

True fellowship with good friends is precious and satisfying like the plentiful overflow of the anointing oil running down from the head of the high priest during his anointing (the other priests were merely sprinkled, but the high priest was drenched). True fellowship is refreshing, like the mountain dew that feeds the springs, and in return supplies the rivers and lakes with water.

Is that psalm a depiction of your life? It isn't likely that you are facing what David was facing. There probably isn't anyone threatening to kill you. Nonetheless, you need authentic community. You need relationships. You need to "live together in unity" with other members of the family of God.

Authentic community can carry you through the toughest of times. It can illuminate your darkness and lighten your burdens. It can deepen and transform you, and it can strengthen and sharpen you as iron sharpens iron. (See Proverbs 27:17.)

Wherever David was when he wrote Psalm 133, he had clearly learned the immeasurable value of unity in community. He had discovered the importance of being surrounded and supported by people who loved God, loved him, and loved each other.

"How good and pleasant it is when God's people live together in unity!" (Psalm 133:1).

Scriptures

Jonathan became one in spirit with David, and he loved him as he loved himself.
—1 Samuel 18:1

How good and pleasant it is when God's people live together in unity! It is like precious oil poured on the head, running down on the beard, running down on Aaron's beard, down on the collar of his robe. It is as if the dew of Hermon were falling on Mount Zion. For there the LORD bestows his blessing, even life forevermore.
—Psalm 133:1–3

Show proper respect to everyone, love the family of believers, fear God.
—1 Peter 2:17

As we have opportunity, let us do good to all people, especially to those who belong to the family of believers.
—Galatians 6:10

Prayer

Father God, thank You for placing me in a community, a family of faith, a church that seeks to honor You by leading me into a closer and stronger relationship with You. Enlarge my love for the family of believers. Deepen my relationships. Broaden them. And walk with me in this thirty-day adventure, using it for my growth and using me for Your glory. In Jesus' name, amen.

Simple Step: A Phone Call

Think through your relationships (maybe seven to ten of your closest friends and family). Is there someone with whom you're not in unity? Is there someone you haven't talked to for a while? Or someone you need to "sharpen" like iron? Set up a time to meet with that friend or family member in person.

Date and initial when you complete this simple step: _____

Journal Prompt

Church isn't a building you go to; it is a family you belong to. Take a few minutes to jot down the ways your church is—or can become—a family to you (for example, "We don't always agree, but we love each other anyway," "We eat together a lot," etc.).

Our church is awsome! allways someone praying, giving hugs, or wanting to help.

Our Monday Bible study is WONDEFUL! We feel free to share our deepest hurts and know they care.

I am so Blessed!

Together Time

Some people are extroverts. They feel comfortable in groups. They tend to be friendly, talkative, and assertive, and they enjoy making new friends. A few hours in the company of others tends to restore and energize them, while solitude can be a draining experience.

Then there are introverts. These individuals are not necessarily shy, nor are they antisocial. They simply feel more comfortable when they are alone than when they are in a group. Typically thoughtful and reserved, they often have many friends. But they are restored and energized by quiet, solitary moments.

Most people fall somewhere between introvert and extrovert. They may lean more in one direction than another, but they are reasonably comfortable both in social situations and periods of solitude. God understands these tendencies. He should, because He created us—all of us—to need alone time *and* together time.

These days, however, it is easy to miss out on both. We may work or drive or eat by ourselves, but these hardly qualify as solitude. And, we may be surrounded by people, though we may not really be "together" with them. The second chapter of Acts, which describes the birth, growth, and dynamic life of the early church, makes frequent references to the followers of Jesus sharing time together:

> *They spent their time learning the apostles' teaching, sharing, breaking bread, and praying together. The apostles were doing many miracles and signs, and everyone felt great respect for God. All the believers were together and shared everything. They would sell their land and the things they owned and then divide the money and give it to anyone who needed it. The believers met together in the Temple every day. They ate together in their homes, happy to share their food with joyful hearts.*
> —Acts 2:42–46 (NCV)

Those first followers of Jesus didn't just go to church on Sunday and greet the folks they knew. Their lives were intertwined. They met together in a large group (in the temple courts) and in small-groups (in their homes). They didn't just share their time; they shared their lives as well.

No matter how long you have been a follower of Jesus, and regardless of whether you are an introvert, extrovert, or something in between, you were created for both solitude and community. In Acts, chapter two, God, who knows you better than you know yourself, provides a snapshot of what your life can look like. He has given you your church family to worship with in a large group setting and share life with in a small-group setting.

That's why the first week of this *30-Day Church Challenge* focuses on community. Just like those first followers of Jesus, we all need to be part of a small-group within the church, so we can experience authentic community through the love, support, and encouragement of others. Such community opens the door to growth and joy in a way that nothing else does.

Scriptures

Peter was kept in prison, but the church was earnestly praying to God for him. The night before Herod was to bring him to trial, Peter was sleeping between two soldiers, bound with two chains, and sentries stood guard at the entrance. Suddenly an angel of the Lord appeared and a light shone in the cell. He struck Peter on the side and woke him up. "Quick, get up!" he said, and the chains fell off Peter's wrists. ... [Then Peter] went to the house of Mary the mother of John, also called Mark, where many people had gathered and were praying.
—Acts 12:5–7, 12

Let us consider how we may spur one another on toward love and good deeds, not giving up meeting together, as some are in the habit of doing, but encouraging one another—and all the more as you see the Day approaching.
—Hebrews 10:24–25

They devoted themselves to the apostles' teaching and to fellowship, to the breaking of bread and to prayer. Everyone was filled with awe at the many wonders and signs performed by the apostles. All the believers were together and had everything in common. They sold property and possessions to give to anyone who had need. Every day they continued to meet together in the temple courts. They broke bread in their homes and ate together with glad and sincere hearts, praising God and enjoying the favor of all the people. And the Lord added to their number daily those who were being saved.
—Acts 2:42–47

Prayer

Lord God, You set the lonely in families (See Psalm 68:6.); and You've given me a church family to enjoy. You provide ways for introverts, extroverts, and those in between to experience authentic community through the love, support, and encouragement of others. Help me to connect and stay connected with my brothers and sisters in Christ, as we grow closer to each other and closer to You. Help me overcome any fear or reluctance and find a group where I can know and be known, love and be loved, celebrate and be celebrated, serve and be served. In Jesus' name, amen.

Simple Step: Search the Church's Website

The church you're attending probably offers fellowship opportunities through small-groups, Sunday-school classes, men's or women's ministries, or groups for young adults or seniors. Look on the church's website, call the church office, or ask someone for information on how you can join a group, class, or ministry. If possible, sign up for a group that is going through the *30-Day Church Challenge* five-week study.

Date and initial when you complete the simple step: _____

Journal Prompt

Look back over Acts 2:42–47, and jot below the parts of their way of life that most appeal to you. Also include some practical ways you might be able to make them a part of your life.

Studying Gods word together
praising God + eating
together

The Great Dance

Gregory of Nazianzus was born sometime around AD 330, during the reign of the Roman Emperor Constantine, who converted to Christianity and decreed that being a Christian was no longer a crime in the Roman Empire. Gregory went to school in Athens, Greece, with a friend named Basil, who would later become the Bishop of Caesarea as well as an important theologian known as "Basil the Great." Gregory himself became Bishop of Sasima and, later, Bishop of Constantinople (named for the Emperor Constantine).

Gregory, Basil, and another friend named Gregory of Nissa, became known as the Cappadocian Fathers, three tremendously influential church thinkers and writers from the same region in what is now central Turkey. Gregory of Nazianzus is famous for being the first person to use the word *perichoresis* to describe the Trinity.

Sounds complicated, doesn't it? But it really isn't.

Perichoresis is a Greek word that literally means "circle dance." If you've ever been to a Greek or Italian wedding (among others), you may have witnessed *perichoresis*. Participants celebrate by linking arms or in some cases, holding handkerchiefs between them as they dance joyfully around and around to the sounds of laughter and loud, happy music. It is also the word Gregory and others used to describe the relationship between God the Father, God the Son, and God the Holy Spirit—a happy dance, a unity, and community. This is evident in Jesus' prayer for His disciples in John 17:

> *My prayer is not for them alone. I pray also for those*
> *who will believe in me through their message, that all*
> *of them may be one, Father, just as you are in me and*
> *I am in you. May they also be in us so that the world*
> *may believe that you have sent me. I have given them*
> *the glory that you gave me, that they may be one as we*

are one—I in them and you in me—so that they may be
brought to complete unity. Then the world will know that
you sent me and have loved them even as you have loved
me.
—John 17:20–23

We were created to reflect God's image (See Genesis 1:26–27.),
and the very nature of God is one of unity in community. Thus, it
is the prayer and will of Jesus that His followers join in the dance.
As C. S. Lewis wrote, "The whole dance, or drama, or pattern of
this three-Personal life is to be played out in each one of us. ...
There is no other way to the happiness for which we were made."
  Our tendency as fallen human beings is to run from God, like
Adam and Eve did in the Garden of Eden (See Genesis 3:8.), and
from community with Him and others. But with our redemption
comes the call—and the indwelling enablement—to live differently, to be better. God wants us to unite with others in community
settings, draw closer to Him and others in small-groups, and reflect the circle dance of God in our relationships with our brothers
and sisters in Christ.
  And, as tends to happen in celebrations that include a circle
dance, the dance gets better as it goes along and the circle widens
to include those who never before suspected that they could dance.

Scriptures

God said, "Let us make mankind in our image, in our likeness, so that they may rule over the fish in the sea and the birds in the sky, over the livestock and all the wild animals, and over all the creatures that move along the ground." So God created mankind in his own image, in the image of God he created them; male and female he created them.
—Genesis 1:26–27

The man and his wife heard the sound of the LORD God as he was walking in the garden in the cool of the day, and they hid from the LORD God among the trees of the garden.
—Genesis 3:8

My prayer is not for them alone. I pray also for those who will believe in me through their message, that all of them may be one, Father, just as you are in me and I am in you. May they also be in us so that the world may believe that you have sent me. I have given them the glory that you gave me, that they may be one as we are one—I in them and you in me—so that they may be brought to complete unity. Then the world will know that you sent me and have loved them even as you have loved me.

"Father, I want those you have given me to be with me where I am, and to see my glory, the glory you have given me because you loved me before the creation of the world.

"Righteous Father, though the world does not know you, I know you, and they know that you have sent me. I have made you known to them, and will continue to make you known in order that the love you have for me may be in them and that I myself may be in them."
—John 17:20–26

Prayer

Righteous Father, though the world does not know You, I know You by Your grace and through Your Son. Thank You for the immeasurable price You paid to redeem me and make it possible for me to join in the fellowship of Your Church. Help me to reflect the unity in community that mirrors Your nature, while I endeavor to model that nature to the world around me. In Jesus' name, amen.

Simple Step: Prayer

Ask God to show you the people connections He wants you to make and guide your steps as you connect with a small-group. If you already have a group you connect with regularly, thank God for them, pray for them, and ask yourself how you can better show them love and support.

Date and initial when you complete the simple step: _____

Journal Prompt

Do you tend to run from communion with God and community with others? Or do you embrace those things? Ponder the question, and then journal a few lines about why you respond the way you do, and what, if anything, you would like to see change.

> I look forward to church and to the group that come to my home. Thank you Lord for each one of them!
> I wouldn't change anything except maybe to add new faces

The Good
and the Not Good

You may have heard that ants can carry fifty times their body weight. If you had that ability, you could lift a Winnebago RV over your head! But did you know that the combined biomass of ants on earth roughly equals the total biomass of all the people on earth?

Ants thrive, at least in part, because they form complex communities. Some ants live in massive "super colonies" that can stretch for thousands of miles. They gather and store food. They communicate and cooperate with each other. And they have much to teach us.

King Solomon, the wisest man in the world during his lifetime said, *"Go to the ant, you sluggard; consider its ways and be wise!"* (Proverbs 6:6). It is a commendation of the ant's work ethic. But that's not the only reason to respect ant ways.

Ants live in community and thrive in community. If there is such a thing as a "solitary ant," it is a rare exception. God created ants to live in colonies. That's where they belong. And yet, the single ant is right at home in the workings of an ant colony. Effective. Healthy. And vibrant. And the same is true of you.

Let's look for a moment at the creation narrative in the Bible book of Genesis. In the beginning of all beginnings, God created light. *"God saw that the light was good,"* the Bible says in Genesis 1:3. Then He created the oceans and the continents, and He said they were good, too. (See Genesis 1:6–10.) Then came vegetation, which was good. (See verse 13.) And the sun, moon, and stars: still good. (See verses 14–18.) He then added sea creatures, flying creatures, land animals of every shape and size, and it was all good. (See verses 21–25.) Then, at last, came the first human being, and "It was very good." (See verse 31.)

It would seem that everything is "good"—until we get to chapter two, that is. "The LORD God said, 'It is not good for the man to be alone. I will make a helper suitable for him'" (Genesis 2:18). That's right, now we're talking "not good."

God had placed one lucky soul in the Garden of Eden, a perfect world. No death, no disease. No conflict, no crime, no crying, no hunger, no hatred, no pollution, politicians, poverty, or pain. It was paradise. That first human being had it all, including intimate, unbroken fellowship with his Creator. And yet, God says it is "not good for the man to be alone." Humanity's first dilemma was not sinfulness; it was aloneness.

You know the rest of the story, of course. God created a woman, a perfect partner for that first man in that pristine place. He recognized that Adam, the first human being, needed companionship with someone else.

You were created—like every other human being on the planet—to need others. Whether you are married or single, young or old, introvert or extrovert, God created you with a desire to live in community. That's where you belong and where you will grow best and thrive most.

Your circumstances and surroundings may be perfect, and yet it is "not good" for you to be alone. You need to be linked to others in healthy, helpful community. Especially with the fast, frenetic lifestyles common in this day and age, connecting with your Christian brothers and sisters in a small-group setting is a great way to help and be helped. A small-group is an ideal place to spur others on toward love and good deeds. It's a place where you can be encouraged and sharpened as you do the same for others. It's a place where "not good" can become "all good."

Scriptures

The LORD God said, "It is not good for the man to be alone. I will make a helper suitable for him."
—Genesis 2:18

Let us consider how we may spur one another on toward love and good deeds, not giving up meeting together, as some are in the habit of doing, but encouraging one another—and all the more as you see the Day approaching.
—Hebrews 10:24–25

A friend loves at all times, and a brother is born for a time of adversity.
—Proverbs 17:17

As iron sharpens iron, so one person sharpens another.
—Proverbs 27:17

Prayer

Loving Father, I know it is not good for me—or others—to be alone. Thank You for showing me—along with the members of my small-group—how to spur others on toward love and good deeds, encouraging and sharpening one another as iron sharpens iron. Teach me to embrace unity in community in both good times and times of adversity. Help me to freely give and receive what Your good, perfect, and pleasing will intends for me and my family of faith. In Jesus' name, amen.

Simple Step: Decide on a Possible Group

If you are not already committed to attending a small-group, visit a small-group or Sunday-school class within the next week.

Date and initial when you complete the simple step: _____

Journal Prompt

The Bible says, *"As iron sharpens iron, so one person sharpens another"* (Proverbs 27:17). Have some areas of your life become rusty and dull? If so, identify them and write down some ways that others can sharpen you in those areas.

Sometimes have trouble trusting God will work everything out in ~~#~~ His time I want an answer ~~at~~ now

"One Anotherness" and You

It's test day in school. The students squirm, and the teacher distributes the test forms and issues one final injunction: "Be sure to read and follow the instructions."

How many students ignored that advice? How many skipped the instructions in an effort to finish more quickly and earned a lower grade as a result? How many of us do the same when it comes to the commands of Scripture?

The New Testament emphasizes "one anotherness." In numerous places, we are instructed to treat "one another" in specific ways. For example:

1. Love one another (John 13:34).
2. Accept one another (Romans 15:7).
3. Be devoted to one another (Romans 12:10).
4. Live in harmony with one another (Romans 12:16).
5. Instruct one another (Romans 15:14).
6. Greet one another warmly (Romans 16:16, 1 Corinthians 16:20).
7. Serve one another (Galatians 5:13).
8. Be patient with one another (Ephesians 4:2).
9. Submit to one another (Ephesians 5:21).
10. Teach and admonish one another (Colossians 3:16).
11. Encourage one another (Hebrews 3:13).
12. Spur one another on toward love and good deeds (Hebrews 10:24).
13. Confess your sins to one another (James 5:16).
14. Offer hospitality to one another (1 Peter 4:9).

We are commanded also to be kind to one another and forgive one another (See Ephesians 4:32.), and to bear one another's burdens (See Galatians 6:2.). And more. Much more.

Some of the "one anothers" in the New Testament are phrased negatively—that is, what we should not do to one another. For example, Romans 14:13 tells us, *"Stop passing judgment on one another,"* and James 4:11 says, *"Do not slander one another."*

It all sounds good, doesn't it? That's how Christians are supposed to act, right? But every single "one another" command assumes a social context. It is impossible to obey those commands unless we are living in community with each other. And that might have been easier—or at least more natural—in the first century, when the early church comprised a network of people meeting in homes, eating together, and sharing each others' lives.

Today, whether your home church consists of a stadium full of people or a handful of people, the context for fulfilling the "one anothers" of Scripture is likely to be a small-group, a class, or home-based gathering. In such a setting, you can rub shoulders with all kinds of people—those who are like you and those who are not. That's a great place to learn how to obey God's commands to love one another, accept one another, bear patiently with one another, and forgive one another.

Trying to fulfill the "one anothers" of Scripture without a small-group community can be much like taking a test without first reading the instructions. You may avoid a little effort at the beginning and even get some things right, but you probably won't grasp and reflect the full purpose of the process. You will miss out. And you will be far less prepared for the next test when it comes.

Scriptures

Carry each other's burdens, and in this way you will fulfill the law of Christ.
—Galatians 6:2

Be kind and compassionate to one another, forgiving each other, just as in Christ God forgave you.
—Ephesians 4:32

Encourage one another daily, as long as it is called "Today," so that none of you may be hardened by sin's deceitfulness.
—Hebrews 3:13

Let us consider how we may spur one another on toward love and good deeds, not giving up meeting together, as some are in the habit of doing, but encouraging one another—and all the more as you see the Day approaching.
—Hebrews 10:24–25

Confess your sins to each other and pray for each other so that you may be healed.
—James 5:16

Above all, love each other deeply, because love covers over a multitude of sins. Offer hospitality to one another without grumbling.
—1 Peter 4:8–9

Prayer

Dear Lord, thank You for the wisdom of Your Word, which guides me to Your will and instructs me in Your ways. Help me to invest myself, my time, and my effort into the community provided by a small-group. Help me also to learn to fulfill the "one anotherness" that You desire for Your people. Let my life be a reflection of the verses above not only in theory but also in practice. In Jesus' name, amen.

Simple Step: An Act of Kindness

Perform one act of service by writing an encouraging note or making a call to a friend you know is going through a difficult time.

Date and initial when you complete the simple step: *9/11/13*

Journal Prompt

In the lines below, journal your answers to these questions: Of the "one anothers" listed in today's reading, which is the most difficult for you? Which is the easiest? Which do you feel you need most from someone else?

Most difficult - instruct
Easiest - love + encourage

From someone else, patience

What a Friend

Jesus was not the only rabbi of His day. In fact, before Jesus came along, the most famous rabbis in Judea and Galilee were Rabbi Hillel, who died when Jesus was a teenager, and Rabbi Shammai, who died about ten years later.

In those days, it was the custom for a young man who wanted to study the Torah (the Hebrew Scriptures) to apply to become one of the rabbi's *talmidim* (followers). If the rabbi agreed, the young man would then shadow the rabbi constantly and absorb his master's teachings, ways of studying and thinking, and lifestyle. Eventually, the best *talmidim* would become rabbis themselves, leaving their teachers in order to teach others.

There are some striking differences between Jesus' relationship with His disciples and the rabbis' relationship with their *talmidim*. For example:

- Jesus' disciples did not apply to Him. He chose each of them personally. He said, *"You did not choose me, but I chose you"* (John 15:16).
- Jesus' *talmidim* did not leave Him in order to become rabbis. He left them so that they would become evangelists: *"After the Lord Jesus had spoken to them, he was taken up into heaven and he sat at the right hand of God. Then the disciples went out and preached everywhere, and the Lord worked with them and confirmed his word by the signs that accompanied it"* (Mark 16:19–20).
- Perhaps most importantly, before leaving His followers to spread His gospel, Jesus told them: *"I no longer call you servants, because a servant does not know his master's business. Instead, I have called you friends, for everything that I learned from my Father I have made known to you"* (John 15:15).

Jesus' relationship with His followers was more than that of rabbi to student; it included a close friendship. Jesus lived His life in relationship with others. He was not only the cousin of John the Baptist but also a close friend. He befriended the lonely and despised Zacchaeus. He was almost certainly friends with "the twelve" before they became His closest disciples. He was criticized for being a friend of tax collectors and sinners. In His darkest hour, in the Garden of Gethsemane, He pointedly asked His closest friends to stay nearby.

Jesus' friendships included the brother-and-sisters trio of Lazarus, Martha, and Mary of Bethany. He visited them frequently in their home, probably lodging there while attending the various feasts at the Temple in Jerusalem. On one occasion at their home, He was asked to referee a dispute between the two sisters. (See Luke 10:38–42.) Another time, as He reclined at the table for a meal, Mary anointed His feet with precious oil and dried them with her hair. (See John 12:3.) And, of course, on another visit, He raised His friend Lazarus from the dead. (See John 11:38–44).

Jesus served as a valuable model for true friendship. A careful reading of the Gospels reveal the nature of a true friend living in community. He fed thousands but He also lingered over meals with friends. He healed all who came to Him but He also raised Peter's mother-in-law from her sickbed. He was Lord of all and yet, He served His friends and washed their feet. He was often heartbroken and ultimately abandoned by many of His friends, but He never let them down. He showed them how to love, forgive, and live in community. And now through the pages of the Bible, He has shown us how to do these things as well.

Scriptures

Jesus went up on a mountainside and called to him those he wanted, and they came to him. He appointed twelve that they might be with him and that he might send them out to preach.
—Mark 3:13–14

As Jesus and his disciples were on their way, he came to a village where a woman named Martha opened her home to him.
—Luke 10:38

Jesus loved Martha and her sister and Lazarus. ... When Mary reached the place where Jesus was and saw him, she fell at his feet and said, "Lord, if you had been here, my brother would not have died." When Jesus saw her weeping, and the Jews who had come along with her also weeping, he was deeply moved in spirit and troubled. "Where have you laid him?" he asked. "Come and see, Lord," they replied. Jesus wept. Then the Jews said, "See how he loved him!"
—John 11:5, 32–36

When he had finished washing their feet, he put on his clothes and returned to his place. "Do you understand what I have done for you?" he asked them. "You call me 'Teacher' and 'Lord,' and rightly so, for that is what I am. Now that I, your Lord and Teacher, have washed your feet, you also should wash one another's feet. I have set you an example that you should do as I have done for you. Now that you know these things, you will be blessed if you do them.
—John 13:12–15, 17

Prayer

Lord Jesus, thank You for Your friendship. You must often be disappointed in me, but You never leave me, nor do You forsake me. Save me from being too shy, self-centered, or busy to establish relationships. Use my relationship, especially those in my small-group, to teach me how to build Jesus-like relationships with others. Help me to love with Your love, forgive with Your mercy and grace, and live in community with Your Spirit of kindness and generosity. In Jesus' name, amen.

Simple Step: Connect with a Friend

Do something with a friend today, even if it's only for five minutes: Make a call. Send a text. Share a cup of coffee. Send flowers. Take a walk together. Or, even better, enlist a friend to connect with another friend!

Date and initial when you complete the simple step: _____

Journal Prompt

The Gospels reveal different sides of Jesus' relationships, from "tax collectors and sinners" to more intimate friendships with people like Mary, Martha, Lazarus, Peter, James, and John. Think about the different kinds of relationships in your life, and how they are being (or could be) used by God for His glory.

I think of my friend Kathy who has parkinsons. We email and encourage each other along our diseased journeys. I plant seeds. Sharon + Tom they do so much for me God is glorified in what they do. Also my sister Sandie

One of the things you discover when you get involved in a really good church is that the church isn't a building you go to, it's a family you belong to. And for every person, the center of family life is usually a small-group that meets regularly so that people can study spiritual truth together. This is a place where each person can know and be known, love and be loved, serve and be served, celebrate and be celebrated.

Community comes with a cost, however. Each person must be willing to invest both time and effort. Each person must choose to be involved in community by listening to others, praying for others, and being a fully invested part of a group that does life together deeply.

Your first weekly challenge, should you choose to accept it, is to join, attend, and contribute to a small-group. You are likely to get the **most** out of this *30-Day Challenge* by doing *three* things:

1. Attend the weekend service so you're up on the subject for the week.
2. Read the daily material in *The 30-Day Church Challenge* book.
3. Be part of a small-group where you can do life and learn truth together.

Some of you may be ready to tackle a bigger challenge: If you are a veteran of small-groups but have never led one, meet with your small-group leader and ask that person to teach you for the next five weeks so you will be prepared to serve as a leader the next time around. Your challenge is to say to your small-group leader, "Would you apprentice me?"

If you are currently leading a small-group, your challenge during these next five weeks is to apprentice at least one member from your group to lead a small-group of their own. If you've never been in a group, your challenge is to show up, contribute by doing your reading, and take a genuine interest in others.

Small-Group Study
and Discussion Questions

For use by small-groups after the Week 1 readings on the topic of Community.

Below is a complete list of small-group study and discussion questions that will cover some of the important themes for this week. We have also included questions regarding the videos that your small-group will watch. In order to stay within the time limits of your small-group meeting, your small-group leader will choose what questions he or she wants your group to focus on. You will need to bring your book with you to your small-group or class.

1. Open in prayer.
2. **Video Stories.** What insights did you gain from watching the video stories by Quay, Ailina, and Justin? How did God speak to you through their testimonies?
3. **Video Stories.** Quay learned that she didn't have to do it all and that other people actually wanted to help her. And she learned to allow people to help her. In what ways can you allow God to use other people in your life this next week. Read Galatians 6:2. Are there burdens you would like to ask our small-group to help you carry?
4. **Video Stories.** Justin spoke about being welcomed and feeling accepted when he visited the church and small-group. What are some specific ways that our small-group can be more welcoming and accepting of others?
5. **Video Stories.** Ailina said that her small-group taught and discipled her (spiritually mentored her). Who are people in your life that could spiritually mentor you? Who are people that you could spiritually mentor?
6. Go around the room asking everyone to briefly answer this question: What is the closest family you've ever seen or been aware of?
7. Read Acts 2:42–47.
8. Ask the question: Do you think the picture of the church in those verses indicates a community that was more intertwined

(Questions continued on the next page.)

with each other's lives than most churches today, less so, or about the same? Why?

9. Ask the question: Do you think those verses reveal the answer to Jesus' prayer in John 17, that His followers would be united in a community like the unity the Father and the Son enjoyed? Why or why not?

10. Ask the question: What do you think would be the effect on the lives of people if their church reflected that kind of community? What would be the effects on the community surrounding the church? How might it affect how your seeking friends, neighbors, and family members view the gospel?

11. Listen to these words from the Day 4 reading in the *30-Day Church Challenge* book: "You were created—like every other human being on the planet—to need others. Whether you are married or single, young or old, introvert or extrovert, God made you to live in community with others. That is where you belong and where you will best be able to grow and thrive." Do you agree with that statement? Why or why not?"

12. Do you think being in close relationship to others makes it easier or harder to follow Jesus? Why?

13. In this week's readings in the *30-Day Church Challenge* book, the following statement was made: "Church isn't a building you go to, it's a family you belong to." Why is that true? Have you seen that in your relationship with the church?

14. Are there any issues holding you back from seeking stronger connections with others in the church? If so, what are they, and what changes would you like to see?

15. What are some ways this group can be a closer and stronger family to you?

16. Name one practical thing this group can do for you, or one specific way we can pray for you in the week ahead.

17. Any other questions or comments?

18. Close in prayer.

WEEK TWO PURPOSE

WORSHIP

Main Message Point: Church is
a great atmosphere to cultivate
a spirit of worship.
God's sacrificial love motivates
us to give all of ourselves
to Him and live our lives
completely for Him. That is
the basis of real worship.

THIS WEEK'S CHALLENGE
Commit to worshiping God by
making regular attendance at
church a cornerstone of your
worship lifestyle and giving
your life completely to Him.

Worship Is a Verb

Imagine yourself among the children of Israel when they arrived at Mount Sinai. Only recently delivered out of slavery, they found themselves approaching a mountain that seemed to be on fire, its topmost height enshrouded by storm clouds, and the voice of God issuing from the mountain like a blast from a giant ram's horn.

What would have been your reaction? Would you have assembled a praise team or sung a few verses of a hymn? Would you have clapped, lifted your hands, or even moved your feet a little bit in worship?

Those are some of the things we label as "worship" today. We speak of "worship leaders" or "worship pastors." We talk about worship as though it is the singing part of our church gatherings. But worship is a verb. It is much more than singing our praises to God. It is more than the hour or two we offer to God on Sundays. And, as the writer to the Hebrews points out, our worship ought to be even greater, more intense, and more pervasive than what the people of Israel experienced at Mount Sinai:

> You have not come to a mountain that can be touched and that is burning with fire" (Hebrews 12:18). "But you have come to Mount Zion, to the heavenly Jerusalem, the city of the living God. You have come to thousands upon thousands of angels in joyful assembly, to the church of the firstborn, whose names are written in heaven.
> —Hebrews 12:22–23

> Through Jesus, therefore, let us continually offer to God a sacrifice of praise—the fruit of lips that confess his name. And do not forget to do good and to share with others, for with such sacrifices God is pleased.
> —Hebrews 13:15–16

As those verses make clear, worship is far more than singing songs during a service. Just as Jesus, the Word that was given for us all on Mount Calvary, is far greater than the words that were given on Mount Sinai, so our worship—as those whose names are written in heaven—should be greater than the worship offered in Moses' day.

Our worship should be a continual "sacrifice of praise." And our sacrifices ought to far exceed a spotless lamb or bull. They should be a day-by-day and moment-by-moment habit of doing good and sharing with others. Acceptable worship for those of us who have come to Mount Zion, who have been saved not by law but by grace, through faith (See Ephesians 2:8) encompasses our whole being. *"Here's what I want you to do, God helping you: Take your everyday, ordinary life—your sleeping, eating, going-to-work, and walking-around life—and place it before God as an offering. Embracing what God does for you is the best thing you can do for him."* (Romans 12:1, MSG). This is the worship that most pleases God.

Scriptures

I urge you, brothers and sisters, in view of God's mercy, to offer your bodies as a living sacrifice, holy and pleasing to God—this is your true and proper worship.
—Romans 12:1

Dear brothers and sisters, I plead with you to give your bodies to God because of all he has done for you. Let them be a living and holy sacrifice—the kind he will find acceptable. This is truly the way to worship him.
—Romans 12:1, NLT

Dear friends, God is good. So I beg you to offer your bodies to him as a living sacrifice, pure and pleasing. That's the most sensible way to serve God.
—Romans 12:1, CEV

Here's what I want you to do, God helping you: Take your everyday, ordinary life—your sleeping, eating, going-to-work, and walking-around life—and place it before God as an offering. Embracing what God does for you is the best thing you can do for him.
—Romans 12:1, MSG

Prayer

Almighty God, I confess that I have long had a limited view of worship. I have worshiped You with singing and prayer, but have too often—and for too long—neglected to truly, properly, and constantly worship You with my life, my body, my "sleeping, eating, going-to-work, and walking-around life." Please enlarge my definition of worship. Deepen my experience of worship. And let everything I learn and do this week be a sweet and pleasing sacrifice to You. In Jesus' name, amen.

Simple Step: A Prayer of Praise

Spend some time talking to God, and as you do, focus on praising Him for who He is and what He has done for you. Be specific.

Date and initial when you complete this simple step: _____

Journal Prompt

On the lines below, brainstorm some ways you can consciously make your "sleeping, eating, going-to-work, and walking-around life" a sacrifice of worship today.

Keeping my eyes on Him. Dying to self and be ready always to testify of His goodness

Wired for Worship

Since the dawn of recorded history, every human culture—no matter how isolated, primitive, or advanced—has worshiped someone or something.

The ancient Persians served a daily ritual meal to their god. The Canaanites worshiped Molech (among others), to whom they offered their children as sacrifices. Egyptians worshiped a hierarchy of gods, dominated from time to time by the sun god Aten or the bull god Apis. The Greeks and Romans worshiped a pantheon of gods. The first North Americans worshiped the sun and other forces in nature. Many African cultures worship one supreme god but recognize other deities as well. And some Asian and African cultures practice the worship of ancestors.

As different as such cultures are from each other, they all illustrate a central fact of human existence: We are wired to worship. The human heart and soul longs to connect with God—even to bow before His greatness—whether it recognizes it or not. Ecclesiastes 3:11 (NLT) says: *"[God] has planted eternity in the human heart,"* and that spark of eternity seeks union with the eternal God. As Augustine wrote in his *Confessions,* "You have made us for yourself, O Lord, and our hearts are restless until they rest in you."

There is no escaping it. You are wired for worship. Your heart, mind, and soul are programmed to reach out to God, bow before Him, praise His greatness, and give yourself to Him in happy surrender and grateful abandon. As C. S. Lewis wrote, "We delight to praise what we enjoy because the praise not merely expresses but completes the enjoyment."

In other words, we are never more ourselves than when we are worshiping God in spirit and truth. We are never closer to the Garden of Eden than when we are walking with God in a continual *"sacrifice of praise"* (Hebrews 13:15), like Adam who walked with God without sin or shame before his Fall. We are never more in tune with the happiness of heaven than when our hearts and souls and lives cry out with the angels and the elders and the four living creatures around God's throne:

> *Amen! Praise and glory*
> *and wisdom and thanks and honor*
> *and power and strength*
> *be to our God for ever and ever. Amen!*
> *—Revelation 7:9–12*

Isn't it true that when a sunset takes your breath away, your soul instinctively rises in worship. When an unexpected blessing comes your way, you naturally want to say thank you. When a thousand little graces permeate your day, your heart's reflex is to praise the God who sent them.

The sin that separated us from God may have short-circuited the natural, instinctive flow of worship from our hearts to God's heart. But the loving sacrifice of Jesus redeems our fallen souls, restores our fellowship with God, reverses our self-centeredness, and returns us to the purpose for which we were created, our "chief end," as the Westminster Shorter Catechism phrased it: "to glorify God and to enjoy him forever."

Scriptures

You are worthy, our Lord and God,
to receive glory and honor and power,
for you created all things,
and by your will they were created
and have their being.
—Revelation 4:11

I looked, and there before me was a great multitude that no one
could count, from every nation, tribe, people and language, stand-
ing before the throne and before the Lamb. They were wearing white
robes and were holding palm branches in their hands. And they
cried out in a loud voice:
"Salvation belongs to our God,
who sits on the throne, and to the Lamb."
All the angels were standing around the throne and around the
elders and the four living creatures. They fell down on their faces
before the throne and worshiped God, saying:
"Amen! Praise and glory
and wisdom and thanks and honor
and power and strength
be to our God for ever and ever. Amen!"
—Revelation 7:9–12

Prayer

Creator God, You are worthy to receive glory and honor and power.
You are worthy to receive the highest praise of my heart and life.
You are worthy to be praised continually. You are worthy to be
thanked for all I have and honored in all I do. You are my King
and my God, and I worship You. In Jesus' name, amen.

Simple Step: A Prayer of Praise

Sometime today, spend five minutes admiring God's creative hand in nature—take a walk, study a tree, pick a flower, watch a bird up close, revel in the sunrise or sunset. Note your heart's response to the beauty you see in creation. Tell God how you feel about it and how you feel about Him.

Date and initial when you complete this simple step: _____

Journal Prompt

Reflect on the last few times you felt sincerely and spontaneously grateful, and use the lines below to record how you responded at those times, and why.

I always cry tears of joy when I think how blessed I am & turn up the music

Begin with Praise

You enter the cavernous concert hall, surrounded by other music lovers. You show your ticket to an usher, who directs you to your row, and you find your seat. The great room is electric with excitement.

Your eyes measure the distance from your seat to the stage. It's closer than you expected. A few musicians wearing black gowns or tuxedos are already seated. Before long, they are joined by others, and soon a delightful cacophony of sound fills the place, as each musician warms up for the program.

Someone enters from the wings with a violin in hand and, standing before the group, plays a single note. That sound is followed by waves of instruments playing the same note.

Finally, the conductor enters, and the crowd applauds. He bows. Turns. Raises a baton. And the music begins.

Whether it's your first such experience, or the latest of many, attending a concert by a symphony orchestra is a unique experience. You may hear a concerto or a sonata, an etude or a suite, but the program typically consists of four movements, the first played "allegro," a musical notation meaning brisk and lively.

In some ways, worshiping God is like a symphony that begins with praise. Focusing on God's praiseworthy attributes serves to orient your heart and mind like a compass pointing to True North. It will set the tone and the direction for the rest of your prayers, your day, your life. Like the first movement of a symphony, praising God will pave the way for whatever themes and melodies may follow.

David, the musician-songwriter-giant killer-king, clearly knew this. He is a model of the worshipful heart and life. He began Psalm 8 with the words, *"O Lord, our Lord, how majestic is your name in all the earth!"* (Psalm 8:1). He started Psalm 18 with, *"I love you, O Lord, my strength,"* and Psalm 19 with, *"The heavens declare the glory of God."* The Twenty-seventh Psalm opens with the words, *"The Lord is my light and my salvation,"* and Psalm

46 begins, *"God is our refuge and strength, an ever present help in trouble."* He made *"Great is the Lord, and most worthy of praise"* the first words of Psalm 48, and his masterpiece, his "magnum opus," commences with *"The Lord is my Shepherd"* (Psalm 23:1).

Worship begins with praise, because praising God's greatness orders the heart and orients the soul. Focusing first on who God is and praising Him for His nature and character affect the sincere heart in four crucial ways:

- **Praising God puts us in our place.** Literally. It exalts God and humbles us—which is the ideal attitude for the worshiping heart.
- **Beginning our worship with praise overcomes our native self-centeredness.** It helps to overcome the common tendency to view our needs, cares, and ideas as most urgent and most important. It reminds us that nothing is greater than God, not even our needs of the moment.
- **Praise changes our perspective.** Truly and sincerely praising the almighty, incomparable God tends to shrink our pain and problems. Praising God's limitless power can also enlarge our vision and dreams, helping us to see that nothing is impossible for God we praise.
- **Praise reminds us that God is God—and we are not.** It can eliminate our need to control things and help us submit to God's control, as we realize the truth of Psalm 100:3–5, which says:

> Know that the LORD is God.
> It is he who made us, and we are his;
> we are his people, the sheep of his pasture.
> Enter his gates with thanksgiving
> and his courts with praise;
> give thanks to him and praise his name.
> For the LORD is good and his love endures forever;
> his faithfulness continues through all generations.

Scriptures

Ascribe to the LORD, you heavenly beings,
ascribe to the LORD glory and strength.
Ascribe to the LORD the glory due his name;
worship the LORD in the splendor of his holiness.
The voice of the LORD is over the waters;
the God of glory thunders,
the LORD thunders over the mighty waters.
—Psalm 29:1–3

Shout for joy to the LORD, all the earth.
Worship the LORD with gladness;
come before him with joyful songs.
Know that the LORD is God.
It is he who made us, and we are his;
we are his people, the sheep of his pasture.
Enter his gates with thanksgiving
and his courts with praise;
give thanks to him and praise his name.
For the LORD is good and his love endures forever;
his faithfulness continues through all generations.
—Psalm 100

Prayer

Heavenly Father, I adore You. I praise You for Your almighty power. I praise You for Your great glory. I praise You for the splendor of Your holiness. I praise You for Your mercy and kindness. I praise You with my whole heart. In Jesus' name, amen.

Simple Step: Make a List

On a piece of paper, write down as many names or attributes of God as you can. For fun, see if you can come up with at least one for each letter of the alphabet.

Date and initial when you complete this simple step: _____

Journal Prompt

What is your "praise default" when your heart turns to praising God? Do you praise Him most often for His power? His love? His grace or His patience? Or for something else? And what (if anything) do you think that "praise default" reveals?

His love + grace

His grace amazes me

The Grateful Heart

Ann's story is certainly not a fairy tale. It is more like a Shakespearean tragedy. When she was a child, her baby sister chased a cat into a farm lane and was crushed under the wheels of a delivery truck. Unable to cope, her mother checked herself into a psychiatric hospital and her father was never the same. A devastating loss like that can mark a family. A life. A soul.

But Ann's story doesn't stop there. Challenged by a friend, she embarked on a daily task of noticing, listing, and giving thanks for the good things she enjoyed each day, no matter how small or routine.

Ann Voskamp's book, *One Thousand Gifts*, in which she tells the story of that challenge and how it changed her life, was an instant best seller. Gratitude is life-changing. And it is an integral part of worship.

Some of the psalms written by David, the shepherd-king of Israel are inscribed, stating that they were written in a particular place or a specific period of his life. But Psalm 103 bears no such inscription. So we have no idea when David wrote this psalm of thanks. It may have been when he was celebrating the return of the Ark of the Covenant to Jerusalem or when he was grieving the death of his infant son. Maybe he wrote it after Bathsheba gave birth to Solomon or while he was fleeing the murderous hand of his rebellious son Absalom. Perhaps it was composed for a court occasion, such as David's coronation or the beginning of his reign in Hebron. Or it may have originated in Jerusalem, after Judah and Israel were united under David's rule. We just don't know.

Maybe it's better that way. After all, the thanks David expresses in this psalm are appropriate for any occasion—much as gratitude is fitting for good times, bad times, and all times in between.

When was the last time you thanked God for forgiving all your sins, healing your diseases, redeeming your life from the pit of hell (or from the pit of depression), or for crowning you with love and compassion? When was the last time you thanked

Him for meeting your needs, satisfying your desires, renewing your strength?

David does all those things—in just the first five verses! Yet we, too often, hold back or tone down our thanks because, well, God hasn't yet healed *that* particular ailment or we still desire more than He has so far given us.

But, as David says, "The Lord works righteousness and justice for all the oppressed." He is compassionate and gracious—all the time. He is slow to anger—all the time. He is abounding in love—all the time. We have much for which we can be thankful, even in the midst of our darkest moments and our most taxing trials.

An ungrateful heart cannot truly worship, because a worshipful life is a grateful life. Maybe that's why we aren't told just when Psalm 103 was written. Because expressing our gratitude to God should not depend on circumstances. Regardless of what situations we might find ourselves in, God remains faithful, for He cannot deny Himself. (See 2 Timothy 2:13.) The greatness of God's love continues to exceed the highest heavens, and the completeness of His forgiveness still extends as far as the east is from the west. Even the broken heart—perhaps, *especially* the broken heart—can give thanks in all circumstances (See 1 Thessalonians 5:18), as Paul the apostle commanded. David did. And Ann Voskamp learned.

Scriptures

Praise the Lord, my soul;
all my inmost being,
praise his holy name.
Praise the Lord, my soul,
and forget not all his benefits—
who forgives all your sins
and heals all your diseases,
who redeems your life from the pit
and crowns you with love and compassion,
who satisfies your desires with good things
so that your youth is renewed like the eagle's.
—Psalm 103:1–5

Praise the Lord, you his angels,
you mighty ones who do his bidding,
who obey his word.
Praise the Lord, all his heavenly hosts,
you his servants who do his will.
Praise the Lord, all his works
everywhere in his dominion.
Praise the Lord, my soul.
—Psalms 103:20–22

Prayer

Thank You, Lord, for all the blessings I enjoy—those for which
I have thanked You repeatedly and those for which I've never
thanked You. I thank You for air and my lungs that allow me to
breathe. I thank You for the food I eat and the taste buds and sense
of smell that enhance my enjoyment. I thank You for your mercies,
which are new every morning, your love that is higher than the
heavens, and your forgiveness that is wider than the distance from
horizon to horizon. Thank You for the mind and spirit and breath
with which to thank You. In Jesus' name, amen.

Simple Step:
Make a "Thank God" List

Make a list of at least ten things you are thankful for today. When your list is complete, read it out loud to God.

Date and initial when you complete this simple step: _____

Journal Prompt

Take a few moments to think about what it is that keeps you from giving thanks. Is it busyness? hardship? something else? Take a few moments to jot down your thoughts about those personal impediments to greater gratitude.

I have learned to be thankful for this disease because it has brought me closer to ~~Jesus~~ Him like I never thought possible

The Joyful Heart

Imagine working your fingers to the bone for your family and fellow countrymen, only to be repeatedly rejected by them. Imagine having to sneak around and stay constantly on the move to escape numerous plots against your life.

Imagine preaching passionately and lovingly in cities large and small, at your own expense, and having the people of faith in those towns—many of them your own flesh and blood—pursue you, slander you, and even imprison you for your trouble.

Imagine enduring exhausting days and sleepless nights, extreme hunger and thirst, bitter cold and brutal heat, while sacrificing for others, many of whom delight in your suffering.

Imagine being mugged by hostile, rowdy mobs and left in the street to die or being deserted by people you thought were your friends. Imagine being involved in a near-fatal accident while being transported to the capital for a politically-charged trial. Imagine taking charge and saving not only your fellow prisoners but also the guards and government officials traveling with you. And imagine, in spite of your exemplary behavior, being delivered nonetheless to a government prison to await trial.

Imagine being broken by years of hardship and suffering, yet continuing to love and pray for all who cross your path.

Does all of that sound to you like a recipe for a worshipful heart?

Surprisingly, it is. All these situations were taken from the life of Paul, the great first-century church planter, who endured beatings and betrayals, shipwrecks, suffering, and disappointment for his faith. This is the same Paul who wrote these words from a Roman prison: *"Rejoice in the Lord always. I will say it again: Rejoice!"* (Philippians 4:4).

Paul's admonition reveals the heart of a true worshiper. Because worship—if it is true worship of the one true God—will be joyful worship.

How is that possible? How can almost constant hardship, rejection, and persecution produce joyful worship? Paul goes on to reveal the secret:

> *Do not be anxious about anything, but in every situation, by prayer and petition, with thanksgiving, present your requests to God. And the peace of God, which transcends all understanding, will guard your hearts and your minds in Christ Jesus. Finally, brothers and sisters, whatever is true, whatever is noble, whatever is right, whatever is pure, whatever is lovely, whatever is admirable—if anything is excellent or praiseworthy— think about such things. Whatever you have learned or received or heard from me, or seen in me—put it into practice. And the God of peace will be with you. I rejoiced greatly in the Lord that at last you renewed your concern for me. Indeed, you were concerned, but you had no opportunity to show it. I am not saying this because I am in need, for I have learned to be content whatever the circumstances. I know what it is to be in need, and I know what it is to have plenty. I have learned the secret of being content in any and every situation, whether well fed or hungry, whether living in plenty or in want. I can do all this through him who gives me strength.*
> *—Philippians 4:6–1*

This passage describes the difference between joy and happiness. Joy is a choice—the overflow of a heart that is focused on God. A joyful heart claims God's promises and focuses on those things that are true, noble, right, pure, lovely, admirable, excellent, and praiseworthy. It gives thanks in every situation and can be content in any circumstance. Joy is both the content and the overflow of a worshiping heart.

Scriptures

Rejoice always, pray continually, give thanks in all circumstances; for this is God's will for you in Christ Jesus.
—1 Thessalonians 5:16–18

Rejoice in the Lord always. I will say it again: Rejoice! Let your gentleness be evident to all. The Lord is near. Do not be anxious about anything, but in every situation, by prayer and petition, with thanksgiving, present your requests to God. And the peace of God, which transcends all understanding, will guard your hearts and your minds in Christ Jesus.
—Philippians 4:4–7

Prayer

I praise You, God and Father of my Lord Jesus Christ! In Your great mercy, You have given me new birth into a living hope through the resurrection of Jesus from the dead, and into an inheritance that can never perish, spoil, or fade. Through faith I am shielded by Your power until the coming of the salvation that is ready to be revealed in the last time. In all this, I greatly rejoice, though for now I suffer grief in all kinds of trials. But I rejoice in that, too, for I know that these have come so that the genuineness of my faith—of greater worth than gold, which perishes even though refined by fire—may result in praise, glory, and honor when Jesus Christ is finally and fully revealed—Him whom I love, though I have not seen Him, and Him whom I believe in, and thus am filled with an inexpressible and glorious joy, for I am receiving the end result of my faith, the salvation of my soul. Amen! (Based on 1 Peter 1:3–9).

Simple Step: Write a Joyful Prayer

Write a prayer to God, using some of the concepts in Philippians 4. Since joy is a choice, identify one circumstance in your life right now where you can *choose* joy, whether or not you *feel* joyful. Tell God about it, and acknowledge that He knows more about your situation than you do.

Date and initial when you complete this simple step: _____

Journal Prompt

Use the lines below to list those things that bring you joy.

My kids
grand + great grandkids
other peoples kids
my dear friends

music

A Lifestyle of Worship

Even in these busy times, people find all sorts of things to do with the moments of their lives. Many people enjoy restoring and showing off their vintage automobiles. You will often see them driving in procession and gathering in parking lots to see and be seen with their coddled cars. Others are model train enthusiasts. They construct elaborate routes through miniature villages, across tiny rivers, and over undersized mountain ranges.

Some people, often referred to as "storm chasers," monitor weather channels on the radio and often drive great distances in the hope of encountering a tornado or severe storm. Some folks prefer to chase ghosts. They spend their spare time taking weekly or monthly jaunts with protective gear and electronic devices intended to help them detect ghosts, orbs, or paranormal activity. Still others opt for tamer pursuits, such as frequenting yard sales and flea markets, riding as many roller coasters as possible, attending sporting events, or crafting their own jewelry.

People who pursue such fancies are as busy as any of their neighbors. They hold down full-time jobs, raise children, pay their bills, and mow their lawns. They simply find ways to incorporate their passions into the rhythm of their daily lives.

Some of the same people attend church. They worship God every week or so. But it apparently never occurs to them that God's good plans for their lives encompasses far more than a weekly dose of worship.

When God delivered His people from slavery in Egypt, He prescribed a pattern for their lives. He commanded a weekly Sabbath, a day of rest and worship and established a series of national festivals for the people to observe. These brought them together for worship every few weeks throughout the year, every year. His people even developed a daily routine of prayers—morning, noon, and night—that integrated well into their agrarian lifestyle.

Very often, our human tendency is to turn romance into routine, and rhythm into meaningless repetition. But worship as God intends it, is not meant to be something we "check off" our to-do list. Worship should not be something that is done merely because it is on our schedule. True worship gets into the blood and finds its way into the rhythms of our daily lives.

God did not prescribe a weekly Sabbath for His people in order to fulfill some cold religious duty. The sacred feasts He commanded were never intended to be routine. They were to be touch points that would keep them in a lifestyle of worship, infiltrating and infecting all the moments of their lives.

How does worship become a lifestyle?

Commit to weekly worship with others. Develop and maintain the habit of meeting together with other worshiping followers of Jesus, as Hebrews 10:25 says: *"[Let us not give] up meeting together, as some are in the habit of doing, but encouraging one another—and all the more as you see the Day approaching.*

Schedule fixed times with God. If morning, noon, and night prayer times are impossible, prioritize at least one daily time and place to be alone with God in prayer, Bible reading, and worship.

Find ways for your weekly and daily routine to intersect with your passion for God. Make your morning commute a time to sing God's praises. Pray while exercising or mowing the lawn. Download an inspiring podcast to listen to on your way to pick up the kids from soccer.

Cultivate a habit of unscheduled worship. Turn off the television and radio sometimes so you can listen to God. Let a sunset prompt a prayer of praise or a siren turn your heart to intercessory prayer for the sick and injured. It may take a little practice, but this will soon become a precious habit and turn your everyday life into a lifestyle of worship.

Scriptures

Remember the Sabbath day by keeping it holy. Six days you shall labor and do all your work, but the seventh day is a sabbath to the LORD your God. On it you shall not do any work, neither you, nor your son or daughter, nor your male or female servant, nor your animals, nor any foreigner residing in your towns. For in six days the LORD made the heavens and the earth, the sea, and all that is in them, but he rested on the seventh day. Therefore the LORD blessed the Sabbath day and made it holy.
—Exodus 20:8–11

Be still, and know that I am God;
I will be exalted among the nations,
I will be exalted in the earth.
—Psalm 46:10

This is what the Sovereign LORD, the Holy One of Israel, says:
"In repentance and rest is your salvation,
in quietness and trust is your strength,
but you would have none of it."
—Isaiah 30:15

[Let us not give] up meeting together, as some are in the habit of doing, but encouraging one another—and all the more as you see the Day approaching.
—Hebrews 10:25

Prayer

Almighty God, so much of what I call "my lifestyle" happens by mistake—or because I've said "yes" to so many other things. But I want to live a life of worship. I want my love for You to invade the days between Sundays. I want to be so passionate about loving You back that worship pervades all my moments, all my days. Make me faithful in weekly worship. Help me fix daily times with You and find ways for worship to intersect with the rhythm of my life, so that worship will overflow and spill into unscheduled moments, too. And help me to start now, today. In Jesus' name, amen.

Simple Step: Listen to God

Take four to five minutes in quiet to listen to a favorite worship song from your music collection or on the web, and then pray your response to the song. Also, commit in your heart to attend church tomorrow.

Date and initial when you complete this simple step: _____

Journal Prompt

Describe some of the best opportunities for worship in your daily and weekly routine and how, if you haven't already, you could turn them into worship.

Like a cell phone is wired for communication, we are wired for worship. And worship is important because we were created to give glory to our Maker. The Bible describes a lot of positive habits that help us give God glory. Gathering for weekly worship is the primary, foundational habit, because it's the one that resets our priorities for the week to come. Hebrews 10:24 starts out by saying: *"Let us not give up meeting together."*

So the challenge this week is to commit to attending weekly worship at least for the rest of this series. Then you can judge for yourself: Do you feel your life is better lived because you're being refueled by God and doing what He's asked you to do?

Having said that, it's important to know that worship is more than attending church on Sunday. It's a verb that describes an action you should engage in with every breath you take. Sunday worship is incredibly important, but from God's perspective, worship is a way of life. Colossians 3:23 says, *"Whatever you do, work at it with all your heart, as if you were working for the Lord and not for a person."* That's worship.

Romans 12:1 (MSG) says: *"Take your everyday, ordinary life— your sleeping, eating, going-to-work, and walking-around life— and place it before God as an offering (an act of worship)."* That's how you worship!

Therefore, the challenge this week is not only to commit to coming to weekly worship every Sunday but also to develop a daily worship lifestyle. We were made to do it and God asks us to do it. In view of who He is and all that He's done for us, how could we do any less?

Small-Group Study
and Discussion Questions

For use by small-groups after the Week 2 readings on the topic of Worship.

Below is a complete list of small-group study and discussion questions that will cover some of the important themes for this week. We have also included questions regarding the videos that your small-group will watch. In order to stay within the time limits of your small-group meeting, your small-group leader will choose what questions he or she wants your group to focus on. You will need to bring your book with you to your small-group or class.

1. Open in prayer.
2. **Video Stories.** What insights did you gain from watching the video stories by Rob and Adam? How did God speak to you through their testimonies?
3. **Video Stories.** Rob discovered that the hole in his life was something that wouldn't be filled by what he could get but only by what he could give. What do you think he meant by that?
4. **Video Stories.** In what way was yelling out a Bible verse from his prison cell an act of worship for Adam?
5. Go around the room asking everyone to briefly answer this question: When is the last time you were speechless or awestruck by something?
6. Read Psalm 150 together.
7. Psalm 150 is the "grand finale" of the Bible's collection of psalms. Why do you think it might have been chosen as the final psalm?
8. Verse 1 says, "Praise the Lord" [Hallelu Yah] and then "Praise God" [Hallelu El]. "Hallelu Yah" occurs many times in the psalms, but this is the first place we see "Hallelu El." Can you think of any reasons for the songwriter to use "Yah" in the first phrase and "El" in the second?[1]

(Questions continued on the next page.)

---

[1] *Adam Clark suggests this is because the two words describe two aspects of God's nature: "Praise Yah, the infinite and self-existent Being; and praise him who is God, El, or Elohim, the great God in covenant with mankind, to bless and save them unto eternal life."*

9. Which verses in this psalm suggest where to worship? Which answer the question, "why worship?" Which mention how to worship? And which discuss who should worship?
10. Of verses 3–5, St. Augustine wrote, "No kind of faculty is here omitted. All are enlisted in praising God." How are the following faculties employed in worship as depicted in verses 3–5?

Breath _____

Fingers _____

Hand _____

Feet _____

Arms _____

Legs _____

Hips _____

Ears _____

Eyes _____

11. How many times does the word "praise" (hallelu) appear in this psalm? Do you think there is any significance to that number? Why or why not?
12. This past week's readings in the *30-Day Church Challenge* book mentioned a few key ingredients of worship—praise, thanks, and joy. Do any of those come more naturally to you than the others? If so, why do you think that is?
13. This past week's readings in the *30-Day Church Challenge* book also talked about cultivating a "lifestyle of worship," in which "your everyday, ordinary life—your sleeping, eating, going-to-work, and walking-around life" is placed before God as an offering. (See Romans 12:1, MSG.) Have you ever tried to do that? If so, how?
14. Do you think God is prompting you to expand your worship, so that it isn't something that happens exclusively on Sundays? If so, how do you think you can do that?
15. Name something you will do this week to worship God with your life.
16. Any other questions or comments?
17. Close in prayer.

WEEK THREE PURPOSE

SPIRITUAL GROWTH

Main Message Point: Growing more like Christ through Bible study, prayer, and attending church enables us to reach our God-given potential.

THIS WEEK'S CHALLENGE

Commit to spending time with God every day.

Like a Cedar of Lebanon

Depending on how you measure it, the largest plant in the world could be the aspen tree, *Populus tremuloides*. An aspen grows in stands of what look like individual trees, but the "trees" are actually stems or ramets that are connected to each other by a common root system. One such aspen plant in the Wasatch Mountains of Utah is known to have produced 47,000 stems covering an area of roughly 110 acres. The entire organism is estimated to weigh more than thirteen million pounds.

Measuring by height, rather than weight or area, the largest plant in the world is the coast redwood *Sequoia sempervirens*, which has been known to climb to a height of 379 feet. This is the size of a thirty-eight story skyscraper.

The world's smallest flowering plant is the *Wolffia globosa*, a rootless plant belonging to the duckweed family. A single wolffia plant is less than 1/42 of an inch long. It weighs about 1/190,000 of an ounce—roughly the same as two grains of table salt. It is so small that five thousand individual plants could be packed into a thimble. The flower produced by each plant is, of course, even smaller, a microscopic pistil and stamen inside a small cavity. The wolffia also produces the world's smallest fruit, which is called a *utricle*. The plant is found in quiet freshwater lakes or marshes around the world.

Large or small, the expansive aspen, giant redwood, and tiny wolffia have one thing in common: they grow. Year by year, season by season, day by day, they grow. That is generally true of all living things, because life involves growth. Sometimes in height, sometimes in depth. Sometimes in girth, sometimes in length. But growth is a function of living things. It is what they do.

The same should be true of God's people. The Bible says: *"The righteous will flourish like a palm tree, they will grow like a cedar of Lebanon"* (Psalm 92:12). The psalmist probably mentioned the palm tree because it is one of the most common and prolific plants that grow in the lands of the Bible. The cedar of Lebanon was the tallest and hardiest of trees the people of the Bible knew. It can attain heights of one hundred feet.

It is God's intention for you to grow. Just as He created the aspen tree to form a root network across many acres and many stems, His intention is for *"your roots [to] grow down into God's love and keep you strong"* (Ephesians 3:17, NLT). Just as God made the *Sequoia sempervirens* to keep growing until it reached the height of a skyscraper, He wants you to *"flourish like a palm tree [and] grow like a cedar of Lebanon"* (Psalm 92:12). And, just as God crafted the tiny wolffia plant to flower and bear fruit, so He designed you to *"bear much fruit, showing yourselves to be [His] disciples"* (John 15:8).

You may not be a redwood or an aspen, spiritually speaking. You may feel more like a wolffia in the grand scheme of things. That's okay, because this *30-Day Church Challenge* is not about imitating anyone else; it is about becoming the best "you" it is possible to be. And "becoming" is just another word for growing. It is about taking steps in the right direction and going from one stage to the next. It is about *"[growing] in the grace and knowledge of our Lord and Savior Jesus Christ"* (2 Peter 3:18), and *"building yourselves up in your most holy faith"* (Jude 1:20, ESV) until you are *"mature and complete, not lacking anything"* (James 1:4).

Scriptures

The righteous will flourish like a palm tree, they will grow like a cedar of Lebanon.
—Psalm 92:12

Let your roots grow down into him, and let your lives be built on him. Then your faith will grow strong in the truth you were taught, and you will overflow with thankfulness.
—Colossians 2:7, NLT

Night and day we pray most earnestly that we may see you again and supply what is lacking in your faith.
—1 Thessalonians 3:10

We ought always to thank God for you, brothers and sisters, and rightly so, because your faith is growing more and more, and the love all of you have for one another is increasing.
—2 Thessalonians 1:3

Grow in the grace and knowledge of our Lord and Savior Jesus Christ. To him be glory both now and forever! Amen.
—2 Peter 3:18

Dear friends, build yourselves up in your most holy faith and pray in the Holy Spirit.
—Jude 1:20

Prayer

Lord God, I want to grow in the grace and knowledge of my Lord and Savior Jesus Christ. Help me to flourish like a palm tree and grow like a cedar of Lebanon. Help me apply myself thoroughly to this *30-Day Church Challenge* so that my roots may grow down deep, my life may be built on the Lord Jesus, my faith may grow strong in the truth, and my life may overflow with thankfulness. In Jesus' name, amen.

Simple Step: Plan for Growth

1. Write out three ways you would like to grow spiritually over the next twelve months.
2. What character trait will you improve on?
3. What negative behavior will you tame?
4. What will you do to stretch yourself spiritually. (This could be a book you read, a retreat you take, etc.).

Date and initial when you complete this simple step: _____

Journal Prompt

Since you've become a follower of Jesus, when did you experience the greatest period of spiritual growth? Was there a time when you grew by leaps and bounds? Was there a time when growth slowed or stopped? What factors do you think contributed to those growing or slowing times?

I grew alot when God moved us to OakHarbor Alliance. It was because of good preaching fellowship & Bible studies. Less growth when we left. More growth again over past year because of the same and because I am learning to get my eyes off me + on Him!

Givers and Takers

Two seas dominated the land where Jesus grew up. One was a scene of beauty, a center of commerce whose shores and depths teemed with life. Fish were abundant in its waters. Carpeted slopes of rich grass encircled this sea. The surrounding countryside was a patchwork of bustling villages and valued farmland. The other sea boasted none of those characteristics. Its shores were barren, the atmosphere harsh, and its bitter waters could not sustain life nor quench thirst.

The difference? One was a *giver* and the other a *taker*.

The Sea of Galilee sparkled with freshness because it not only received the water that flowed down from the northern mountains but also gave itself to the winding Jordan River as it flowed to the south.

The Dead Sea received fresh water daily from the Jordan River, but kept it all. All the sediment and minerals halted their flow within its boundaries.

This principle of giving and taking applies to people as well as bodies of water. In fact, the contrast between those two bodies of water may have been in Jesus' mind when He told His earliest followers, *"Whoever believes in me, as Scripture has said, rivers of living water will flow from within them"* (John 7:38).

Givers notice the needs of others. They tend to ask, "How can I help?" They are quick to pitch in and lend a hand. They often pick up the tab. They ask sincere questions. They love people and use things, not the other way around. They listen well and get their hands dirty. They give easily and generously—even sacrificially, at times—to the needs of others.

Takers, on the other hand, are often oblivious to the needs of those around them. They tend to think in terms of, "What's in it for me?" They don't like to go out of their way and may feel resentment if they have to change their plans. They are sensitive to their own rights. They are prone to love things and use people, rather than the other way around. They tend to talk more than they listen.

They avoid people and situations that might ask too much of them. And they often reason that they have far too many needs or plans of their own to worry about someone else's.

The person who is always taking and never giving will become stale, unpleasant, and bitter—like the Dead Sea. Because growth is closely related to giving, takers tend to stagnate and decline over time.

However, men and women who freely give of themselves—their attention, possessions, time, and effort—will as surely become sweet, pleasant, and refreshing. Givers often experience rapid personal and spiritual growth because they are constantly sharing with others and making room in their lives for more blessing, new discoveries, and increased capacity.

It is quite simple, really. God cannot give more to those whose hands are already full.

Scriptures

A generous person will prosper; whoever refreshes others will be refreshed.
—Proverbs 11:25

Whoever believes in me, as Scripture has said, rivers of living water will flow from within them.
—John 7:38

Give to everyone what you owe them: If you owe taxes, pay taxes; if revenue, then revenue; if respect, then respect; if honor, then honor. Let no debt remain outstanding, except the continuing debt to love one another, for whoever loves others has fulfilled the law.
—Romans 13:7–8

Let us not become weary in doing good, for at the proper time we will reap a harvest if we do not give up. Therefore, as we have opportunity, let us do good to all people, especially to those who belong to the family of believers.
—Galatians 6:9–10

Prayer

Father, make me a giver. Save me from selfishness and self-centeredness. Teach me to give to everyone what I owe, whether that is respect, honor, gratitude, attention, consideration, love, or something else. Help me to do good to all people and especially to those who belong to the family of believers. Let rivers of living water flow from within me and spill out of my life, refreshing all those around me. In Jesus' name, amen.

Simple Step: Be a Giver, Not a Taker

Practice being a giver by challenging yourself to give more than you take in every conversation and relational exchange today.

Date and initial when you complete this simple step: _____

Journal Prompt

Who are the most giving people you know, past or present? Write about the ways you are like—or unlike—them. Come up with some practical ideas for how you can give even more.

My Dad, + sister

Tom + Sharon

Debra + Jeremy

The Mark of Maturity

Regardless of how old you are, there was probably a time in your life when you couldn't wait to grow up. When you were a toddler, you wanted to get old enough to cross the street by yourself. Or maybe you longed for the day when you would no longer be forced to take naps. Or you may have anxiously anticipated your first day of school, or the day when you would be as tall as a sibling or cousin.

Those longings may have changed over the years, but they probably didn't disappear. As you got older, you may have dreamed of becoming a teenager, entering high school, or getting your driver's license.

After that, you may have yearned to leave home and go off to college. Then you may have anticipated grad school or the start of your first "real" job. At some point, you might have dreamed of the day when you would fall in love, get engaged, and marry.

And so it goes. Many people view such moments as mileposts on the road to adulthood. Some, however, reach those points and still don't feel "grown up." Some even raise children, and go on to become grandparents, while continuing to feel not-quite-mature.

When is the point at which a boy becomes a man? When does a girl become a woman? When is a "kid" no longer a kid but an adult?

Biologically speaking, that question is a fairly easy one to answer. An organism is considered an "adult" when it is able to reproduce. From flowers and trees to birds and bees, this is true of all living things. And it is also true when it comes to spiritual growth.

Too often, followers of Jesus believe that worshiping regularly with other believers demonstrates maturity. Of course, that's an important ingredient for growth. But it is not the mark of maturity.

Others see themselves as mature because they consistently read and study their Bibles. They memorize verses and meet with others to study together. That, too, is an important factor in spiritual growth. But it is not the mark of maturity.

Some think they have reached spiritual maturity when they are able to fill a valuable role of service to the church. Others feel they have reached spiritual maturity because they have been a Christian longer than anyone they know. Some feel they've arrived when the pastor asks them for advice. But none of these is the mark of spiritual maturity.

Jesus said, *"I am the vine; you are the branches. If you remain in me and I in you, you will bear much fruit"* (John 15:5). Later in that same talk with His disciples, He said, *"I chose you and appointed you to go and bear fruit—fruit that will last"* (John 15:16).

Like branches on a grapevine or another fruit-bearing plant, we have been chosen and appointed—watered, fed, and tended—to bear fruit, to reproduce, to play a part in repeating over and over again the process that produced our salvation. That is the mark of maturity. That is how we know that the Holy Spirit's work and our cooperation have combined in us to produce a full-grown follower of Jesus.

In fact, it is not going too far to say that we were born to reproduce. That's right. Every step we have taken, every little bit we have grown, has been largely for the purpose of reproducing. You are fulfilling the Father's plans for you only if you are bearing fruit and reproducing (John 15:1–2).

Growing in grace and in the knowledge of our Lord Jesus Christ is not something we do to make ourselves look or feel better. It's something the Holy Spirit does in us so that the gospel will spread throughout the world. (See Colossians 1:6.)

Scriptures

I am the vine; you are the branches. If you remain in me and I in you, you will bear much fruit; apart from me you can do nothing.
—John 15:5

I chose you and appointed you to go and bear fruit—fruit that will last.
—John 15:16

I planted the seed, Apollos watered it, but God made it grow.
—1 Corinthians 3:6

In the same way, the gospel is bearing fruit and growing throughout the whole world—just as it has been doing among you since the day you heard it and truly understood God's grace.
—Colossians 1:6

Prayer

Heavenly Father, thank You for Your kindness You've shown me by bringing me into fellowship with You through Your Son, Jesus Christ. Thank You also for giving me a place among the redeemed and patiently tending and caring for me, like a gardener in a vineyard. Thank You for those who planted the seed of faith in me and for those who watered it. Thank You for the fruit their efforts have produced. Help me grow up and produce much fruit, both in the way I live and in playing a part in the salvation of many. I know I can only do this by Your grace and by abiding in and relying on Your Son. In Jesus' name, amen.

Simple Step: Pray for a Friend

Who do you know that should be part of God's family, but isn't? Begin praying that God would use you as part of His plan to bring that person into His family.

Date and initial when you complete this simple step: _____

Journal Prompt

Unlike the biological process of attaining maturity, the task of becoming a reproducing follower of Jesus does not depend on your age. It is a matter of submission, trust, and obedience more than development. Are there fears or insecurities that keep you from taking those steps toward maturity? If so, what are they? If not, what can you do now to *"go and bear fruit that will last"* (John 15:16)?

A Daily Time with God

If you started this *30-Day Church Challenge* book on day one, you have now completed half of the journey! Congratulations. Chances are, in the past fifteen days, you've hit a few bumps in the road. Maybe you missed one day or even two. Maybe you've even started to lose some of your initial enthusiasm for the journey.

Don't give up. Let this day—just past the halfway mark—be a renewal of your commitment to see this project through to the end. After all, you do want to experience all the benefits, don't you?

It's possible to get so busy in life that you lose sight of where you're going—like the pilot in World War II who was flying over the Pacific Ocean when he radioed back to his headquarters, "I'm lost. I have absolutely no idea where I'm going. But I'm making record time."

That's right. You can be making good time, but if you've forgotten where you're going—and why—it makes little difference. A daily time with God can fix that. It can re-orient you. It can re-energize you. In fact, talking to God in prayer and letting Him talk to you from His Word is essential to spiritual growth.

It's easy to let your daily time with God become a source of guilt or stress. But it doesn't have to be three hours on your knees by your bedside. It can be fifteen minutes over a cup of coffee. It can be ten minutes on the way to work in the morning. It can be five minutes every night—after your twelve children are in bed.

Whatever it may look like for you, a daily time with God for prayer and Bible reading is vitally important. The Bible says, *"Jesus often withdrew to lonely places and prayed"* (Luke 5:16). Jesus was a plenty busy guy for His day and time. He had places to go—on foot, no less—people to see, people to heal, people to teach, people to raise from the dead, not to mention His volunteer work at the Five Loaves and Two Fishes Soup Kitchen!

Yes, Jesus was a busy man, but He still "often withdrew" because His time with His Father was His source of strength and energy. Don't you think you need strength at least as much as Jesus did? If anything, you need it more—we all do.

To get started, try these suggestions:

Choose a time. Select a daily time to meet with God, one you can realistically keep. Put it on your calendar. Set a reminder on your phone or computer. If you've been reading this book and writing in this journal at the same time every day, it's probably a good idea to make that your chosen time.

Find a place to withdraw. Jesus "withdrew to lonely places," where interruptions and distractions were unlikely and He could be alone with His Father. You should identify some place to pray and read the Bible that is away from distractions like the television. You might even want to find a place without cell-phone reception.

Have a plan. It doesn't have to be complicated. It may be five minutes of praise and thanks, followed by five minutes of Bible reading, and ending with five minutes of letting your requests be made known to God. Or you may listen to a worship song on your iPod, then spend a few minutes in silence before alternating a few moments of prayer with a few minutes of reading. Your plan can be anything you want it to be. The important thing is that you *have* a plan!

Stick to it. For most people, it takes roughly twenty-one days to form a habit. If you carve out daily time with God for twenty-one days in a row, you are likely to be amazed at the growth you experience and the changes it brings about in your heart, mind, and life.

Scriptures

Be still, and know that I am God; I will be exalted among the nations, I will be exalted in the earth.
—Psalm 46:10

Keep this Book of the Law always on your lips; meditate on it day and night, so that you may be careful to do everything written in it. Then you will be prosperous and successful.
—Joshua 1:8

In the morning, LORD, you hear my voice; in the morning I lay my requests before you and wait expectantly.
—Psalm 5:3

My soul yearns for you in the night; in the morning my spirit longs for you.
—Isaiah 26:9

Open my eyes that I may see wonderful things in your law.
—Psalm 119:18

All Scripture is God-breathed and is useful for teaching, rebuking, correcting and training in righteousness.
—2 Timothy 3:16

Prayer

Almighty God, my Father, forgive me for acting as though I need Your presence and power less than my Lord Jesus Christ did. Make me hungrier for You and Your Word than I have ever been before. Help me to carve out times to be still and know that You are God. Help me to rejoice in You and keep Your Word always on my lips, meditating on it day and night, for I know this is the way to become prosperous and successful in Your eyes. In Jesus' name, amen.

Simple Step: Begin a Daily
Quiet Time with God

Ask God to help you establish a daily quiet time. Make a commitment to read the Bible for at least ten minutes a day for the rest of the *30-Day Church Challenge*. If you need help choosing a reading plan, ask your pastor or small-group leader for advice. In addition, a selection of Bible reading plans are available at www.biblegateway.com.

Date and initial when you complete this simple step: _____

Journal Prompt

What do you think would change in regard to your life and your spiritual growth if you made it a point to get away from the busyness of your life and pray? What practical difference do you think it would make if the Word of God was "always on your lips," and you meditated on it *"day and night, so that you may be careful to do everything written in it"* (Joshua 1:8)?

I've seen prayers answered

feel closer to the Lord

God speaks to me

The Things Prayer Does

If we really knew the things that prayer accomplishes, we would *"pray constantly"* as it says in 1 Thessalonians 5:17. A casual glance through the pages of the Bible shows a little of what prayer can accomplish:

Abram's prayer produced a son.
Jacob's prayer preceded reconciliation with his brother.
Moses' prayers delivered a nation from slavery.
Moses' prayer prevented a nation's destruction.
Israel's prayers brought manna from heaven.
Joshua's prayer resulted in victory.
Gideon's prayers routed oppression.
Manoah's prayer brought guidance from God.
Hannah's prayers gave her a child.
David's prayers restored his relationship with God.
Solomon's prayer blessed him with wisdom.
Elijah's prayer caused a drought.
Elijah's prayer raised a widow's son from the dead.
Elijah's prayer brought down fire from heaven.
Elijah's prayer ended a drought.
Elisha's prayer raised a widow's son from the dead.
Ezra's prayers revived a nation.
Nehemiah's prayer gained him favor in the sight of a king.
Daniel's prayer shut the mouths of lions.
Jonah's prayer saved him from the belly of the whale.
Mary's prayer made her the mother of the Messiah.
The leper's prayer brought healing.
The Roman centurion's prayer saved the life of his servant.
The prayer of two blind men restored their sight.
Peter's prayer while walking on the Sea of Galilee saved him from drowning.

Jesus' prayer in Gethsemane brought ministering angels to his side.

The apostles' prayers resulted in the Day of Pentecost.

Peter's prayer raised Dorcas from the dead.

Cornelius's prayers brought about the Gentile Pentecost.

The Jerusalem church's prayers delivered Peter from prison.

Paul's prayer healed the governor of Malta.

Can you believe it? This is a partial list! A comprehensive list of what prayer accomplished just for the people whose stories are recorded in the Bible would be a book in itself. Little wonder, then, that James wrote, *"Is any one of you in trouble? He should pray. ... Is any one of you sick? He should call the elders of the church to pray"* (James 5:13–14).

American preacher and author E. M. Bounds once wrote, "God does nothing but in answer to prayer." Prayer is the means by which God heals. It is through prayer that God opens prison doors and saves lives. Through prayer, He brings about reconciliation and victory. Through prayer, He frustrates oppressors, bends the will of tyrants, sends rain on the earth, and dispatches angels. It is through prayer that God calms storms and raises the dead.

These are the kind of things that tend to come to mind when we read James' words, *"The prayer of a righteous person is powerful and effective"* (James 5:16). Prayer changes things. But that isn't all prayer does.

Prayer also changes us.

One reason the prayer of a righteous man or woman is powerful and effective is because prayer changes the person who prays. Prayer emboldened the timid Gideon and transformed him into a mighty warrior. Prayer healed and restored David's heart and life after his sin with Bathsheba. Prayer will bring about more leaps of growth and heights of joy in your life than you would ever have thought possible.

If you truly believe the Bible, you will believe what it says about prayer. And if you believe what it says about prayer, you will *"pray continually"* (1 Thessalonians 5:17) for all the circumstances of your life and the lives of others.

Scriptures

Jesus said to them, "Suppose you have a friend, and you go to him at midnight and say, 'Friend, lend me three loaves of bread; a friend of mine on a journey has come to me, and I have no food to offer him.' And suppose the one inside answers, 'Don't bother me. The door is already locked, and my children and I are in bed. I can't get up and give you anything.' I tell you, even though he will not get up and give you the bread because of friendship, yet because of your shameless audacity he will surely get up and give you as much as you need.

"So I say to you: Ask and it will be given to you; seek and you will find; knock and the door will be opened to you. For everyone who asks receives; the one who seeks finds; and to the one who knocks, the door will be opened."
—Luke 11:5–10

Pray continually.
—1 Thessalonians 5:17

Call to me and I will answer you and tell you great and unsearchable things you do not know.
—Jeremiah 33:3

When you pray, do not keep on babbling like pagans, for they think they will be heard because of their many words. Do not be like them, for your Father knows what you need before you ask him.
—Matthew 6:7–8

Prayer

Lord Jesus, as Your first disciples asked, I ask also: Teach me to pray. Endow my prayers with the faith of Abraham, the perseverance of Hannah, the boldness of Elijah, the humility of David, the wisdom of Solomon, the courage of Daniel, the desperation of Jonah, the submission of Mary, and the audacity of Peter. Help me pray and refuse to give up, for the honor of Your Name, and the spread of Your kingdom. In Jesus' name, amen.

Simple Step: Experiment with Journaling

Journal one prayer a day—even if it's just a single sentence—until you reach the end of this challenge. You may want to conclude your journal entry in this book with a prayer each day or write your daily prayers in a separate journal. Seize this opportunity to experience prayer journaling. You can decide when you've completed the challenge if you want to continue or not.

Date and initial when you complete this simple step: _____

Journal Prompt

What prayers would you pray right now if you truly believed that "God does nothing but in answer to prayer?" Record them below.

Daniel
my Jake

Finding a Barnabas

Paul was not always an apostle. The Bible relates how, soon after Paul had become a follower of Jesus, a man named Barnabas, whose name means "son of encouragement" took Paul under his wing. He introduced Paul to the leaders of the Jerusalem church, paving the way for the former persecutor of Christians to be accepted by the apostles. Sometime later, when the apostles sent Barnabas to lead the burgeoning church in Antioch, Barnabas recruited Paul to help him teach the growing multitude of Christ-followers in Antioch. (See Acts 11:25–26.)

We know Paul as the indefatigable apostle to the Gentiles, the great church planter of the first century, and the author of fourteen books in the New Testament. But all that came after Paul was mentored by Barnabas.

What Barnabas did for Paul, Paul later did for others—most notably in the case of his younger protégé Timothy.

Paul and Timothy probably met on Paul's first missionary journey, which he made with Barnabas. Timothy apparently became a follower of Jesus as a result of Paul's ministry, and Paul described him in his letters as his beloved and faithful son in the Lord (See 1 Corinthians 4:17), and as his *"true son in the faith."* (See 1 Timothy 1:2.) Later, when Paul returned to Lystra, where Timothy lived, he recruited Timothy as Barnabas had once recruited him. (See Acts 16:1–5.) Years later, when Paul wrote to Timothy from a Roman prison, probably within weeks of the elder man's martyrdom, he was still offering guidance to his protégé in the challenging assignment of leading the church at Ephesus.

Barnabas and Paul weren't the only ones. The Apostle John mentored a young man named Ignatius, who became the Bishop of Antioch. John also taught a young man named Polycarp, who became the Bishop of Smyrna. Polycarp then mentored Irenaeus, who became the Bishop of Lyons. The Apostle Peter taught Clement, who became the Bishop of Rome. It is no coincidence that these individuals are among the most revered in church history. Having the right mentor can result in amazing growth and development in a person's life.

A mentor can teach you things you might not otherwise learn and take you places you could not otherwise go. A mentor is usually older and always more experienced, at least in the areas in which you wish to be mentored. An effective mentor is someone you would enjoy spending time with and at the same time, someone who is not afraid to offer constructive criticism or hold you accountable.

Your church or pastor may be able to help you find a suitable mentor. If you prefer to find a mentor on your own, try this:

Humble yourself. Make sure you are approaching a mentoring relationship with a humble, teachable attitude.

Identify the things you want to learn from a mentor. What are the graces you would like to develop? The skills you hope to acquire? The accomplishments you would like to pursue?

Choose someone you admire and respect. This should be someone who has matured to a place you would like to be, someone who might be willing to encourage, guide, and coach you to get there.

Ask. Contact your potential mentor and ask him or her to consider meeting with you on a regular basis. Be prepared to discuss how the relationship might work, how often you would like to communicate. Would it be weekly, monthly? If your mentor is hesitant, suggest a trial period. You may want to agree that either of you can end the relationship at any time with no hard feelings.

Keep trying. Don't be surprised or disappointed if you don't succeed right away. Finding the right fit is often a process of trial and error. Don't give up. As Barnabas, Paul, and Timothy's case illustrates, a good mentoring relationship can have a huge impact on you—and on the kingdom of God.

Scriptures

The Spirit told Philip, "Go to that chariot and stay near it." Then Philip ran up to the chariot and heard the man reading Isaiah the prophet. "Do you understand what you are reading?" Philip asked.

"How can I," he said, "unless someone explains it to me?" So he invited Philip to come up and sit with him.
—Acts 8:29–31

Paul, an apostle of Christ Jesus by the will of God, in keeping with the promise of life that is in Christ Jesus,
To Timothy, my dear son:
Grace, mercy and peace from God the Father and Christ Jesus our Lord.

I thank God, whom I serve, as my ancestors did, with a clear conscience, as night and day I constantly remember you in my prayers. Recalling your tears, I long to see you, so that I may be filled with joy. I am reminded of your sincere faith, which first lived in your grandmother Lois and in your mother Eunice and, I am persuaded, now lives in you also.

For this reason I remind you to fan into flame the gift of God, which is in you through the laying on of my hands. For the Spirit God gave us does not make us timid, but gives us power, love and self-discipline.
—2 Timothy 1:1–7

The things you have heard me say in the presence of many witnesses entrust to reliable people who will also be qualified to teach others.
—2 Timothy 2:2

Prayer

Lord God, open my heart and mind to the benefits and blessings of a mentoring relationship. Help me identify a possible mentor. Give me humility and wisdom in planning for such a relationship. And lead me into a partnership with a mentor that will bear fruit in my life for Your glory. In Jesus' name, amen.

Simple Step: Think and Pray About a Mentor

Pray about who could serve as your mentor, using the guidelines offered above. Note: Your responsibility is to bring questions and to be responsive. When you recruit your mentor, be sure to clarify that you aren't asking that person to make you grow but to help you grow. If your mentor recognizes something he or she wants to do to help you grow, that's great, but otherwise, be prepared to take the initiative by asking questions.

Date and initial when you complete this simple step: _____

Journal Prompt

Write down a few names of possible mentors and their strengths below. Which of these will you commit to approaching about spending time together in a mentoring relationship?

The goal this week is to grow spiritually by committing to take one spiritual step at a time. And this week's weekly challenge is to commit to spending time with God every day for prayer and Bible reading. You speak to God when you pray. God speaks to you while you're reading the Bible.

If reading the Bible is new for you, challenge yourself to read for at least five minutes a day for the next twenty-one days. It takes twenty-one days to build a habit, so this will help greatly in your effort to make daily Bible reading a constant in your life. And either before or after reading the Bible, spend two minutes talking to God in prayer. Your prayers don't have to be elaborate. Simply tell God what you're thinking and how you'd like His help during your day.

If you have never read the Bible from beginning to end, the book of Luke is a good place to start. From there you can continue to read through the end of the New Testament. Challenge yourself to read for five minutes a day. You won't get through the whole thing in twenty-one days, but you should commit to reading for at least that long.

You really can grow to be like Jesus when He was here on earth. But to do so, you'll have to change your thinking. That's why Paul says to be "transformed by the renewing of your mind." It's vital to establish a habit of reading God's thoughts.

If you already spend time reading the Bible and praying each day, seven minutes probably won't be much of a challenge for you. Consider setting your goal at fifteen minutes. Soon you'll want to spend even more time talking to your heavenly Father and letting Him talk to you. Combine that with the other challenges you're taking during these thirty days, and you'll be on the road to becoming the person God created you to be!

Small-Group Study
and Discussion Questions

For use by small-groups after the Week 3 readings on the topic of Spiritual Growth.

Below is a complete list of small-group study and discussion questions that will cover some of the important themes for this week. We have also included questions regarding the videos that your small-group will watch. In order to stay within the time limits of your small-group meeting, your small-group leader will choose what questions he or she wants your group to focus on. You will need to bring your book with you to your small-group or class

1. Open in prayer.
2. **Video Stories.** What insights did you gain from watching the video stories shared by Julia and Cyrus? How did God speak to you through their testimonies?
3. **Video Stories.** Cyrus shared how God's Word has taught him and how the words in the Bible are life. What lessons has the Word of God taught you? Share one important verse, and what it has taught you. Be brief so that everyone in the group will have an opportunity to share.
4. **Video Stories.** Though she didn't start that way, Julia said that she now spends all day in constant dialogue with God. How can you incorporate more prayer into your daily life?
5. Go around the room asking everyone to briefly answer this question: Some people have a green thumb. Others seem better at killing plants than growing them. Which more accurately describes you?
6. Read 1 Thessalonians 5:16–24.
7. In 1 Thessalonians 5, the Apostle Paul gave final instructions to Christians living in and around the Greek city of Thessalonica. Which of his instructions in those verses speaks most directly to you, and why?

(Questions continued on the next page.)

8. In verse 24, Paul says, *"The one who calls you is faithful, and he will do it."* Do you think Paul is saying that we don't have to do anything to *"grow in the grace and knowledge of our Lord and Savior Jesus Christ"* (2 Peter 3:18)? Why or why not?

9. What sort of things can followers of Jesus do to encourage the work of God in their lives and build themselves up in their most holy faith? (See Jude 1:20.)

10. This past week's readings in the *30-Day Church Challenge* book suggested several steps we can take to grow stronger as followers of Jesus: daily prayer and Bible reading, a lifestyle of giving rather than taking, reaching out to others, and finding a mentor. Have you decided to pursue any of these steps?

11. Can you think of a period in your life when you grew more spiritually than you have recently? If so, when was it, and what was different about that period of time compared to now?

12. If you had to choose one area in which you would like to grow spiritually over the next twelve months, what would it be, and why?

13. If you had to choose one area of your spiritual life in which you would like to grow *this month*, what would it be, and why?

14. Name one practical way you can start that growth process this week.

15. Any other questions or comments?

16. Close in prayer.

WEEK FOUR PURPOSE
STEWARDSHIP

Main Message Point: When
you faithfully manage the
resources (time, talents, and
treasures) God has given you,
He blesses you and uses you to
change the world.

THIS WEEK'S CHALLENGE
Commit to increasing your
stewardship through giving
and serving.

Of Children and Kings

It is a normal stage in the growing process. A child, sooner or later, learns the significance of the word "mine."

Gina was surrounded by a dozen friends and family members at her second birthday party. Each guest had entered with a package wrapped in colorful paper. When her mother sat Gina down amid all the packages, the little girl's joy knew no bounds. With Mom's help, she opened one gift after another and clutched it to her chest, apparently fearing that someone would take it from her. "Mine!" she said, over and over.

Drew retreated to his bedroom when his cousins came to visit. He closed the door and refused to play with them. When his father stepped into the room, Drew started crying. Eventually, the source of Drew's distress was revealed. He didn't want his cousins playing with his toys. "Mine," he said.

When Marie's parents decided it was time to replace her toddler bed with a big girl bed, she suffered an emotional crisis. Stomping her feet and screaming at her parents, she pointed to the bed and screamed, "Mine!" She pointed to her toys and screamed, "Mine!" She pointed to the floor and walls of the bedroom and screamed, "Mine!"

Gina, Drew, and Marie are children, of course. They are still learning. But their attitudes are not as childish as we may think. Human, yes. But childish, no.

When God created the first human, he *"took the man and put him in the Garden of Eden to work it and take care of it"* (Genesis 2:15). The garden didn't belong to the man. He was the manager of its many wonders.

When God prepared His people, Israel, to enter and occupy the Promised Land, He commanded them: *"The land must not be sold permanently, because the land is mine and you reside in my land as foreigners and strangers. Throughout the land that you hold as a possession, you must provide for the redemption of the land"* (Leviticus 25:23–24).

When King Nebuchadnezzar, a pagan ruler, looked from the window of his royal palace in Babylon and admired all the beauty and majesty of his capital city, he said, *"Is not this the great Babylon I have built as the royal residence, by my mighty power and for the glory of my majesty?"* (Daniel 4:30).

Before the words had fully escaped his mouth, God sent judgment on the king. Nebuchadnezzar became like a wild animal, eating grass and letting his hair and fingernails grow. After seven years, he regained his senses and asserted God's dominion, not his own, saying: *"His dominion is an eternal dominion; his kingdom endures from generation to generation"* (Daniel 4:34).

We are prone to the error of Nebuchadnezzar. We humans tend to think we are owners when God has repeatedly made it clear that we are managers.

The Bible says, *"The earth is the Lord's, and everything in it"* (Psalm 24:1). Everything we possess has come from Him; *"It is he who gives you the ability to produce wealth,"* as Deuteronomy 8:18 says. Whatever wealth or comfort we enjoy belongs to us in the same way that little girl's bed belongs to her. It is nothing more than a flawed perception. No matter how loudly she may scream, "Mine," she did not buy the item in question and cannot keep it without her parents' approval.

The same is true of everything we have and enjoy. Our lives, our homes, and all our "stuff" is a trust from God—the same God who bought us with the lifeblood of His Son.

He owns it all. No matter how loud we may scream, "Mine."

Scriptures

The earth is the LORD's, and everything in it, the world, and all who live in it; for he founded it on the seas and established it on the waters.
—Psalm 24:1–2

Remember the LORD your God, for it is he who gives you the ability to produce wealth, and so confirms his covenant, which he swore to your ancestors, as it is today.
—Deuteronomy 8:18

To the LORD your God belong the heavens, even the highest heavens, the earth and everything in it.
—Deuteronomy 10:14

Prayer

Dear God, the earth is Yours, and everything in it—the world, and all who live in it. You own me. You own my life. You own my home, my possessions, my clothes, and my car. Thank You for entrusting these things to my care. Help me to consciously and consistently treat them as a trust from You, managing them and accounting for them according to Your instructions. In Jesus' name, amen.

Simple Step: Identify Who Owns What

Take a pad of sticky notes and write "God's" on each one of them. Then go around your house and place one on each item, acknowledging in a very hands-on way that everything you have belongs to God.

Date and initial when you complete this simple step: _____

Journal Prompt

Nebuchadnezzar was humbled by God because he arrogantly believed and asserted that he had made *himself* great. Which of your "possessions" do you think you are most attached to? Which are you most tempted to take credit for? Why?

Treasures Are a Test

Money does supernatural things to us and in us—and for us. Jesus once said, *"Where your treasure is, there your heart will be also"* (Luke 12:34).

Notice the order of those words: Where your treasure is … your heart will be also. That is not how we usually *hear* those words. We tend to think Jesus said, "Where your heart is, that is where you will put your treasure." Or, as many preachers and writers have put it, "If you want to know where your heart really is, take a look at your checkbook."

What Jesus really said is this, "Where you put your treasure, that is where your heart will be." The order of the words is not accidental. The sequence is important. That is how it works, according to Jesus. If you put your treasure some place, your heart will follow. Maybe sooner. Maybe later. But make no mistake: Where your treasure is, your heart will be.

This means that money is not a trap; it's a test. The Bible warns us never to say, " *'God is trying to trip me up.' God is impervious to evil, and puts evil in no one's way"* (James 1:13, MSG).

But money is a test. Always. Treasure is a test. Possessions are a test. Everything you own is a test. A test of your affection. A test of your devotion. A test of your trust.

It is powerful, but dangerous—like the ring in J. R. Tolkein's most famous books, *The Hobbit* and the Lord of the Rings trilogy. The ring's mysterious power enslaved the tragic Gollum, and nearly subdued Frodo, who barely managed to pass the test and escape a similar fate.

God may use money and possessions to prepare you for something. He may use them to warn you or reveal something to you about the state of your heart, the depth of your faith, or the extent of your trust in Him. Sometimes God uses money and possessions to teach the same lessons over and over—because you haven't yet passed the test or taken the lesson to heart.

Think about it. What might the following questions reveal about your attitudes toward money:

Do you pride yourself on your income?
Do you feel superior or inferior to others because of what you earn or what you own?
Do you waste money?
Do you hoard money?
Do you use money more to reward yourself? To express love to others? To worship God?
Do you view financial blessing as a gauge of God's favor?
Does a financial setback prompt you to question God's love, wisdom, or power?
Are you quick to help others in need?
Since Jesus says, "Where you put your treasure, that is where your heart will follow," what does your spending *today* indicate about where your heart will be in the future?

What would change in your life if you actively put Jesus' words into action and determined to put your treasure where you want your heart to be? How would your spending be different? How would your investments change? How would it affect your giving?

According to Jesus, your spending today has a direct correlation to where your heart will be tomorrow. The only question is, will you pass the test?

Scriptures

Where your treasure is, there your heart will be also.
—Luke 12:34

Whoever can be trusted with very little can also be trusted with much, and whoever is dishonest with very little will also be dishonest with much. So if you have not been trustworthy in handling worldly wealth, who will trust you with true riches? And if you have not been trustworthy with someone else's property, who will give you property of your own?
—Luke 16:10–12

His master replied, "Well done, good and faithful servant! You have been faithful with a few things; I will put you in charge of many things. Come and share your master's happiness!"
—Matthew 25:21

It is required that those who have been given a trust must prove faithful.
—1 Corinthians 4:2

Prayer

Lord Jesus, I confess that I have often failed the test in my attitudes and actions regarding money. But I want to be a good and faithful servant. I want to pass the test. Help me to seriously and conscientiously consider where I am putting my treasure and my trust. Let me make whatever changes need to be made so that my heart will follow hard after You, and not after the things of this world. In Jesus' name, amen.

Simple Step: Consider a Budget

- Choose one of the following for today's step:
- Draft a realistic spending plan that reflects your financial—and spiritual—priorities.
- Give away something you own as a way of releasing your grip on your possessions or theirs on you and as a way to bless someone else.
- Go to Christian personal finance instructor Dave Ramsey's website at www.daveramsey.com and decide when and where you, (and your spouse) will enroll in a Financial Peace course.

Date and initial when you complete this simple step: _____

Journal Prompt

Turn back to the questions listed in today's reading. Choose the question that hits closest to home for you and write out your thoughtful response in the space below.

_____

_____

_____

_____

_____

_____

_____

_____

_____

_____

_____

_____

Everyone Tithes

Would it surprise you to know that you tithe? You may not even know what that word means. It's simple really. A tithe is just an old word for ten percent. It was used in the Bible to refer specifically to the practice of giving the first ten percent of your income— whether crops from your fields, livestock from your herds, income from your business, or wages from your job—to God.

"Well," you might say. "I don't do that." But whether you know it or not, you are a faithful tither. In fact, everyone you know—every single soul, male or female, young or old, rich or poor, churchgoer or not—is a faithful tither. Why? Because *everyone* tithes the first ten percent of his or her income—their paycheck, tips, business receipts, dividends, royalties, etc.—somewhere. It goes to something. Or someone.

Some people tithe to the credit card company. Others tithe to the bank for the loan on their speedboat. Some tithe to the liquor store, others to Starbucks. Some tithe to the shoe store or the bookstore. But the first ten percent of everyone's income goes somewhere.

We just don't all tithe to God.

It was as true in ancient times as it is today. It was as true of Israel as it is of the church you attend. And it really does hurt God's feelings. The prophet Malachi wrote:

"Will a mere mortal rob God?" [says the Lord Almighty.] "Yet you rob me."

"But you ask, 'How are we robbing you?'

"In tithes and offerings. You are under a curse—your whole nation— because you are robbing me. Bring the whole tithe into the storehouse, that there may be food in my house. Test me in this," says the Lord Almighty, "and see if I will not throw open the floodgates of heaven and pour out so much blessing that there will not be room enough to store it. I will prevent pests from devouring your crops, and the vines in your fields will not drop their fruit before it is ripe," says the Lord Almighty.

—Malachi 3:8–11

That Bible passage reveals several striking truths:

- **Giving a tithe to something or someone other than God is robbing God.** From the days of His earliest revelation to humanity, God made it clear that the first fruits, the firstborn, the first ten percent of His people's income was to be given to Him. It all belongs to Him anyway; He simply asks His people to give a tithe to indicate their awareness of that truth.

- **God invites His people to test His generosity by tithing.** This is the only time God allowed an exception to the command in Deuteronomy 6:16, which says, "Do not put the Lord your God to the test." This is the only area in which God allows us to test Him—which ought to indicate how important this promise is.

- **God indicates that robbing Him invites a curse, but tithing invites immeasurable blessings.** God doesn't need our money. Giving Him the tithe is a matter of obedience. It puts God—and money—in their proper places. When we give back to God what He has asked of us in the form of the tithe, we bring blessing to the people of God.

Scriptures

No one can serve two masters. Either you will hate the one and love the other, or you will be devoted to the one and despise the other. You cannot serve both God and money.
—Luke 16:13

"Return to me, and I will return to you," says the LORD Almighty. "But you ask, 'How are we to return?' "Will a mere mortal rob God? Yet you rob me. "But you ask, 'How are we robbing you?' "In tithes and offerings. You are under a curse—your whole nation—because you are robbing me. Bring the whole tithe into the storehouse, that there may be food in my house. Test me in this," says the LORD Almighty, "and see if I will not throw open the floodgates of heaven and pour out so much blessing that there will not be room enough to store it. I will prevent pests from devouring your crops, and the vines in your fields will not drop their fruit before it is ripe," says the LORD Almighty.
—Malachi 3:7–11

Prayer

Father, I want to be obedient. I want to please You. I want to worship You alone. I want to put You—not money or possessions—on the throne of my life. Help me to show my true colors, my real priorities, by giving You a tithe of all You have given me. In Jesus' name, amen.

Simple Step: Experiment with Tithing

Take the Ninety-Day Tithe Test by giving ten percent of your income from each paycheck to your local church for the next ninety days. At the end of the test, decide whether God has been faithful enough for you to continue. If you are already tithing, pray about becoming a Kingdom Contributor. This is someone who gives at least $100 a month above the tithe to your church.

Date and initial when you complete this simple step: _____

Journal Prompt

Jesus said, *"No one can serve two masters. Either you will hate the one and love the other, or you will be devoted to the one and despise the other. You cannot serve both God and money"* (Luke 16:13). How does your spending and giving habits reflect those words?

Wealth that Wins
a Welcome

If an angel appeared to you tonight to tell you that you would die tomorrow, what would you do?

Would you go out and buy a new pair of shoes? Would you get your hair done? Would you ask your boss for a bonus? Would you try to spend all the money in your bank account?

You probably wouldn't do any of those things, would you? You would likely realize that those things lose their importance when you have twenty-four hours or less to live. Right? So, how would your answer change if you had, say, forty-eight hours? Or seventy-two hours? Would your answer change if you had a week or a month? Probably not. Money and possessions lose their value in the light of eternity.

That was the point of one of Jesus' parables. It is a story that some consider the most confusing tale He ever told. It goes like this:

> There was a rich man whose manager was accused of wasting his possessions. So he called him in and asked him, "What is this I hear about you? Give an account of your management, because you cannot be manager any longer."
>
> The manager said to himself, "What shall I do now? My master is taking away my job. I'm not strong enough to dig, and I'm ashamed to beg—I know what I'll do so that, when I lose my job here, people will welcome me into their houses."
>
> So he called in each one of his master's debtors. He asked the first, "How much do you owe my master?"
>
> "Nine hundred gallons of olive oil," he replied.
>
> "The manager told him, 'Take your bill, sit down quickly, and make it four hundred and fifty.'
>
> Then he asked the second, "And how much do you owe?"

"A thousand bushels of wheat," he replied. He told him, "Take your bill and make it eight hundred."

"The master commended the dishonest manager because he had acted shrewdly. For the people of this world are more shrewd in dealing with their own kind than are the people of the light. I tell you, use worldly wealth to gain friends for yourselves, so that when it is gone, you will be welcomed into eternal dwellings."

—Luke 16:1–9

Jesus was not commending dishonesty in that parable. He was promoting proper priorities. His parable conveys four key truths:

- **We will soon be called to give an account.** Like the steward in the story, most of us could be accused of wasting our Master's possessions. And whether we live one more day, another year, or another twenty years, our day of reckoning approaches faster than we know.

- **This impending reckoning reveals how irrelevant the hoarding of money and possessions is.** All the wealth we have accumulated—whether it is little or much—is shown to be worthless in light of the approaching end of this earthly life. Like Confederate currency in the waning days of the Civil War, it has no real value.

- **It is not too late to change.** The steward in Jesus' story changed his attitude and behavior in light of his master's message. We still have time to change ours.

- **Wealth used to bless others is not wasted.** Like Ebenezer Scrooge on Christmas morning, the shrewd steward learned a new use for money. Instead of hoarding it, he turned it to a new purpose. Similarly, because we, as people of God, know that only two things on earth are eternal— God's Word and human souls—we would be wise to focus our resources on those things.

Scriptures

I tell you, use worldly wealth to gain friends for yourselves, so that when it is gone, you will be welcomed into eternal dwellings.
—Luke 16:9

Command them to do good, to be rich in good deeds, and to be generous and willing to share. In this way they will lay up treasure for themselves as a firm foundation for the coming age, so that they may take hold of the life that is truly life.
—1 Timothy 6:8

Prayer

Lord God, thank You for reminding me that money and possessions are worthless in light of eternity, and it is up to me to put them to eternal use. Help me win a glorious welcome for myself and others into Your eternal kingdom by the purposes to which I apply the wealth You entrust to me here on this earth. In Jesus' name, amen.

Simple Step: Use Your Skills

Identify a way to use your time, talent, and treasure to open a door or build a friendship with someone who could someday welcome you into eternal dwellings. Could you serve someone by helping them change their oil? Could you take dinner to someone who is sick? Perhaps you could pay a visit to someone who is elderly and rarely gets out of the house. Be creative!

Date and initial when you complete this simple step: _____

Journal Prompt

Take a few moments to reflect on the parable of the shrewd steward. When it comes to managing money, how are you *like* that steward? In what ways are you *unlike* him? How will you use your time, talent, or treasure to build a friendship with someone you know who doesn't go to church?

The God of the Open Hand

Imagine overhearing a conversation like this between God and the angels on the fifth day of Creation:

ANGEL: Pardon me for asking, Lord, but why are you doing all this?

GOD: I am creative by nature. Why do you ask?

ANGEL: Well, it just seems like—forgive me for saying— overkill. I mean, You have already created more than ten billion galaxies. Seventy sextillion stars—that's a number seven with twenty-two zeroes after it!

GOD: I am aware of that. I also created math.

ANGEL: Right. Sorry about that. But You've created ten times as many stars as all the grains of sand on all the world's beaches and in all the world's deserts.

GOD: Don't you like it?

ANGEL: Like it? Sure! It's amazing. But that's just the beginning. You have planted more than twenty thousand different kinds of trees. And 270,000 different kinds of flowers.

GOD: I know. Can you guess how many varieties of orchid I made?

ANGEL: But that's my point.

GOD: You think it's too much.

ANGEL: Does the earth really need, what, four-thousand-plus kinds of mammals? Ten thousand different bird species? More than twenty thousand kinds of fish? And a couple thousand types of fruit? I know it is Your nature to create, but—

GOD: And tomorrow I will create the first human. I will breathe life into him. And all this will be his to enjoy—the stars, the flowers, the fruits, the birds. I will tell him, "This is all for you. Have fun."

ANGEL: Won't he be overwhelmed?

GOD: I expect he will. He will be grateful, too. And happy. But that is not the primary reason for all this. It is simply my nature to be generous.

ANGEL: Well, I have to give You that.

This is an imaginary conversation, of course. But it makes a point. The God of Creation is the God of the open hand. Psalm 145:16 says of Him, *"You open your hand and satisfy the desires of every living thing."* And Psalm 33:5 (MSG) says, *"Earth is drenched in God's affectionate satisfaction."* In fact, God's Word teaches:

- **Generosity is godly.** God's limitless, extravagant generosity is an aspect of His nature. And it ought to be a model for us. We may beg God to make us rich or at least comfortable; but He urges us to become generous, like Him.
- **If God blesses us, it is so that we can be more generous.** A lot of us think, "I would give a lot more to God's work if I had it to give." But the Bible says God supplies seed to sowers, not to hoarders. (See 2 Corinthians 9:10–11.) And He does it so that we "will be enriched in every way so that you can be generous on every occasion" (2 Corinthians 9:11).
- **Generosity invites blessing.** Some people think that if we give generously to God, He will give us a yacht or a mansion or a Mercedes-Benz E-Class but that just shows what we really love. The Bible says that if we give cheerfully and generously, *"God is able to make all grace abound to you, so that in all things at all times, having all that you need, you will abound in every good work"* (2 Corinthians 9:8). God does not promise to bless us so we can be richer than we ever dreamed. He promises to bless us so we can be more generous than we ever thought possible.

That, of course, is an accurate reflection of God's generous nature, and therefore in keeping with the way God's kingdom operates: When God blesses a man, a woman, a family, a church, or a nation, He blesses them so they can be a blessing to others.

Scriptures

Remember this: Whoever sows sparingly will also reap sparingly, and whoever sows generously will also reap generously. Each of you should give what you have decided in your heart to give, not reluctantly or under compulsion, for God loves a cheerful giver. And God is able to bless you abundantly, so that in all things at all times, having all that you need, you will abound in every good work.
—2 Corinthians 9:6–8

He who supplies seed to the sower and bread for food will also supply and increase your store of seed and will enlarge the harvest of your righteousness. You will be enriched in every way so that you can be generous on every occasion, and through us your generosity will result in thanksgiving to God.
—2 Corinthians 9:10–11

Give, and it will be given to you. A good measure, pressed down, shaken together and running over, will be poured into your lap. For with the measure you use, it will be measured to you.
—Luke 6:38

Prayer

Gracious and generous Father, I want to be like You. Because of the surpassing grace You have given me, I want to be among those who sow generously, not sparingly. I want to be a cheerful giver. I want to abound in every good work. I want to be generous on every occasion, that my generosity may result in thanksgiving to You. Teach me generosity that I may supply the needs of Your people and bring about joy and thanksgiving to You. Thank You, Father, for giving Jesus, Your indescribable gift. In Jesus' name, amen.

Simple Step: Share Something

Thank God for His generosity, and the goodness He showers on your life. Try "paying it forward" today by coming up with a creative way to give something anonymously (pay for the person behind you in line at the coffee shop or drive through, feed an expired parking meter, etc.).

Date and initial when you complete this simple step: _____

Journal Prompt

Which is your greatest challenge when it comes to becoming more like your generous God: giving *generously* or giving *cheerfully*? Do you have trouble trusting that God will restore your supply? Or is there something else you struggle with? Whatever your answer, ask yourself why that is difficult for you.

Flour and Oil, Bread and Fish

A poor widow once trudged outside the city gate to gather a few sticks for a cook fire on which to prepare a meal for herself and her son. It would be their last. There was no more food in the house and no way to get any more in a land devastated by drought. She would have cried had there been any moisture or strength left in her body. As she worked, a traveler called to her and asked for a cup of water and a piece of bread. She said she had just enough flour and oil to cook a final meal for herself and her son. The man told her to go home and fix that meal—but first to make a small loaf of bread for him. He promised in the name of the Lord that if she followed his instructions, her jar of flour and jug of oil would not run out. The widow did as the man asked and found that he was indeed a prophet for her supply was never exhausted.
—Based on 1 Kings 17:7–16

A destitute widow once came to the prophet Elisha. She told him that the bill collectors would soon be coming, and she had nothing in the house but a little oil. Her two sons would surely be conscripted as slaves to pay her debts. The prophet told her to collect as many jars as possible and start filling them up with the oil from her almost empty jar. The oil filled every jar she could put her hands on. It kept coming and coming, providing enough income for her to pay her debts.
—Based on 2 Kings 4:1–7

A man once came to Elisha with twenty loaves of barley bread. Elisha said to hand out the bread to a crowd of one hundred men who were standing nearby. The man protested that the twenty little loaves would not be nearly enough, but he did as the prophet said. Even after all the men ate their fill, there was bread left over.
—Based on 2 Kings 4:42–44

It was getting late. Jesus, the rabbi from Galilee, had been teaching all day, and the crowd had continued to grow. Jesus' disciples grew worried for the hungry crowd. They looked around for food to share but found only a boy with a modest lunch—five loaves and two small fish. The boy offered his lunch to Jesus, who took it, blessed it, and gave it to His disciples to distribute to the crowd of thousands. The food kept coming. And coming. And everyone ate. The food left over was more than the initial supply.

—Based on Mark 16:30–34

Each of these incidents, recorded in the Bible, shows the gracious and plentiful provision of our loving God. In each case, the people in the story were acutely aware of their need, but they mistakenly assumed that their supply came only from natural sources. They could see that their resources were hopelessly limited. And they also assumed—quite naturally—that once they started giving away what they had, it would be gone in short order.

All their assumptions were proven wrong. Unlike the prophets Elijah and Elisha, and unlike Jesus, their eyes were focused on the scantiness of their earthly resources, rather than the generous provision of their heavenly Father.

Jesus said, *"I tell you, do not worry about your life, what you will eat or drink; or about your body, what you will wear. Is not life more than food, and the body more than clothes? Look at the birds of the air; they do not sow or reap or store away in barns, and yet your heavenly Father feeds them"* (Matthew 6:25–26).

The God who miraculously replenished a widow's supply can provide for all your needs. The God who delivered another widow from debt can deliver you as well. In fact, He can take *whatever* you put in His hands—whether one hundred loaves or five—and multiply it, meeting not only your needs but also the needs of those around you.

Scriptures

"Therefore I tell you, do not worry about your life, what you will eat or drink; or about your body, what you will wear. Is not life more than food, and the body more than clothes? Look at the birds of the air; they do not sow or reap or store away in barns, and yet your heavenly Father feeds them. Are you not much more valuable than they? Can any one of you by worrying add a single hour to your life?

"And why do you worry about clothes? See how the flowers of the field grow. They do not labor or spin. Yet I tell you that not even Solomon in all his splendor was dressed like one of these. If that is how God clothes the grass of the field, which is here today and to-morrow is thrown into the fire, will he not much more clothe you—you of little faith? So do not worry, saying, 'What shall we eat?' or 'What shall we drink?' or 'What shall we wear?' For the pagans run after all these things, and your heavenly Father knows that you need them. But seek first his kingdom and his righteousness, and all these things will be given to you as well."
—Matthew 6:25–33

My God will meet all your needs according to the riches of his glory in Christ Jesus.
—Philippians 4:19

Prayer

God, I confess that my eyes are too often focused on my need and my scant natural resources. I tend to overlook the fact that your heavenly provision is plentiful. Heal my unbelief. Give me the vision of Elijah, Elisha, and Jesus Himself, and teach me to trust You to provide, even when—especially when—the need is great. Help me to place all my resources in Your hands, and give You the opportunity to multiply them, according to Your wisdom and love. In Jesus' name, amen.

Simple Step: Make an Altar

Place a loaf (or even a crumb) of bread and a small container of oil someplace where you will see it every day throughout this next week. Think of it as a reminder to you of God's faithful provision in your life.

Date and initial when you complete this simple step: _____

Journal Prompt

Take a few moments to think back and consider. Then list as many specific examples as you can of how God has blessed and provided for you.

_____

_____

_____

_____

_____

_____

_____

_____

_____

_____

_____

_____

_____

_____

_____

_____

_____

This week's challenge is to increase your stewardship through giving and serving. Take a few moments and give serious thought to this question: *What will you do with the things entrusted to you?* Your time, talents, and treasure are not actually yours. God gave you life, so your time belongs to Him. God gave you talents; they're on loan from Him. God gave you the capacity to earn money, and all that you earn ultimately comes from Him because you're the manager and He's the Master.

Do you remember the late-night, public-service announcement that used to come on television? The station would put on its logo and say, "This is a test. This is only a test." After a few seconds they would say, "This has been a test of the Emergency Broadcast System. If this had been an actual emergency, you would have been instructed to turn to your emergency channel."

How are you doing with the money test? If you've never given, give your first donation to the church this week and see what happens. If you're a sometimes-giver, decide to become a regular giver. If you're a regular giver, determine to give the full tithe. If you're a tither, find a way to excel at the grace of giving.

Remember, too, that stewardship is not just about money. You have time and talents that could be used by God to greatly encourage others. It could be that you can do the kind of construction work that's always needed at your church. Or maybe you love working with children and could help train them for God. Or you may have a knack for computers and could help with multimedia and online ministry. Or it could be that you have a knack for making people feel welcome and could serve as a greeter or usher.

Wherever you are in terms of managing your time, talents, and treasure, take a step forward in terms of your stewardship.

Small-Group Study
and Discussion Questions

For use by small-groups after the Week 4 readings on the topic
of Stewardship.

Below is a complete list of small-group study and discussion
questions that will cover some of the important themes for this
week. We have also included questions regarding the videos that
your small-group will watch. In order to stay within the time limits
of your small-group meeting, your small-group leader will choose
what questions he or she wants your group to focus on. You will
need to bring your book with you to your small-group or class.

1. Open in prayer.
2. **Video Stories.** What insights did you gain from watching the
   video stories by Jim and Jennifer? How did God speak to you
   through their testimonies?
3. **Video Stories.** Jim shared examples of people who selflessly
   volunteered their time to join something bigger than themselves. What church project or ministry in the church would
   you prayerfully consider volunteering your time, talents, or
   treasure to help with?
4. **Video Stories.** Jennifer shared all that God did when she let go
   and started trusting Him with her finances. What has God done
   for you as you've let go and trusted Him with your finances?
5. Go around the room asking everyone to briefly answer this
   question: Who is the most generous person you've ever known
   or met?
6. Read 2 Corinthians 9:6–15.
7. In this passage about giving, why do you think Paul uses
   "sowing" and "reaping" as a metaphor?
8. By talking about "sowing" and "reaping" in regard to money,
   do you think Paul is saying, if you give $100 to God, you will
   reap $1,000 or $10,000? Why or why not?
9. What do you make of the four "alls" in verse 8?
10. How does verse 9 make the point that those who give are like God?

(Questions continued on the next page.)

11. According to verse 10, does generosity affect righteousness? Or does righteousness affect generosity?
12. According to verse 11, for what purposes does God bless generous people?
13. According to this passage, how many different kinds of results are produced by generosity? (See especially verses 6, 8, 10–14.)
14. Listen to these words from the day twenty reading in the *30-Day Church Challenge* book: "God may use money and possessions to prepare you for something, warn you, or reveal something to you about the state of your heart, the depth of your faith, or the extent of your trust in Him. Sometimes, God uses money and possessions to teach the same lessons over and over—because you haven't yet passed the test or taken the lesson to heart." Has God ever used money and possessions to prepare you for something? to warn you? or to reveal something to you?
15. Complete this sentence: I think I would be more generous if _____.
16. Do you tend to be more generous in times of blessing or times of need? Why do you think that is?
17. Name one way you could cooperate with God this week to supply the needs of His people, producing an overflow of thanks to Him. (See 2 Corinthians 9:12.)
18. Any other questions or comments?
19. Close with a period of prayer, giving thanks to God for Jesus, His indescribable gift. (See 2 Corinthians 9:15.)

WEEK FIVE PURPOSE

OUTREACH

Main Message Point: God has
called us to share the good
news of the gospel through our
words, our love, and our lives.

THIS WEEK'S CHALLENGE
Commit to sharing your faith
with someone or reaching out
by inviting them to church.

To Seek and to Save

In July, 1941, there was an escape from the cruel concentration camp at Auschwitz, in Poland. It was the custom at Auschwitz to kill ten prisoners for every one who escaped. All the prisoners would be gathered in the courtyard, and the commandant would randomly select ten names from the roll book. These victims would be immediately taken to a cell where they would receive no food or water until they died.

One after another, as the commandant called the names, the doomed prisoners stepped forward. The tenth name he called was a man named Gajowniczek. He stepped forward, but was unable to stifle his sobs. "My wife and children," he said softly, over and over.

Suddenly there was a movement among the prisoners. The guards raised their rifles. The dogs tensed, anticipating a command to attack. An eleventh prisoner left his row and pushed his way to the front. He was told to stop or be shot. He stopped a few paces from the commandant, removed his hat, and looked the German officer in the eye.

"Herr Commandant," he said, "I wish to make a request, please. I want to die in the place of this prisoner." He pointed at the sobbing Gajowniczek. "I have no wife or children. Besides, I am old and not good for anything. He is in better condition."

"Who are you?" the officer asked.

"A priest."

The commandant hesitated for a moment, then barked, "Request granted."

Prisoners were not allowed to speak, but Gajowniczek said later, "I could only thank him with my eyes. I was stunned and could hardly grasp what was going on. The immensity of it: I, the condemned, am to live because someone else willingly and voluntarily offered his life for me—a stranger."

The priest's name was Maximilian Kolbe. He died a few weeks later, in the punitive cell. But Gajowniczek survived the war and lived more than fifty-three years after Kolbe died for him.

Gajownikczek's story is our story and the story of every soul living on this earth. We were the prisoners, marked for death until Jesus stepped forward and took our place. Jesus saved us by willingly and decisively giving up His life so that we might live.

Jesus explained His Great Condescension in the simplest terms: *"The Son of Man came to seek and to save the lost"* (Luke 19:10). He compared Himself, metaphorically, to a shepherd who seeks a lost lamb, a housewife who searches for a precious family heirloom, and a father who runs to welcome back his wandering son.

According to Scripture, God reconciled us to Himself through Christ. *"He has committed to us the message of reconciliation. We are therefore Christ's ambassadors, as though God were making his appeal through us"* (2 Corinthians 5: 18–20).

If you are a follower of Jesus, God has called you to share the good news of the gospel through your words, your love, and your life. Every follower of Jesus is called to follow His example by seeking out those who haven't yet experienced new life in Christ. We are to *"Go into all the world and preach the gospel to all creation"* (Mark 16:15). Not all of us are called to be preachers; but we are all commanded to spread the good news of the gospel. Not all of us are engaged in full-time ministry; but we have all been given the ministry of reconciliation. Not all of us are natural evangelists; but we are all Christ's ambassadors.

Scriptures

Jesus came to them and said, "All authority in heaven and on earth has been given to me. Therefore go and make disciples of all nations, baptizing them in the name of the Father and of the Son and of the Holy Spirit, and teaching them to obey everything I have commanded you. And surely I am with you always, to the very end of the age."
—Matthew 28:18–20

He told them, "This is what is written: The Messiah will suffer and rise from the dead on the third day, and repentance for the forgiveness of sins will be preached in his name to all nations, beginning at Jerusalem. You are witnesses of these things."
—Luke 24: 46–48

He said to them, "Go into all the world and preach the gospel to all creation."
—Mark 16:15

If anyone is in Christ, the new creation has come: The old has gone, the new is here! All this is from God, who reconciled us to himself through Christ and gave us the ministry of reconciliation: that God was reconciling the world to himself in Christ, not counting people's sins against them. And he has committed to us the message of reconciliation. We are therefore Christ's ambassadors, as though God were making his appeal through us. We implore you on Christ's behalf: Be reconciled to God. God made him who had no sin to be sin for us, so that in him we might become the righteousness of God.
—2 Corinthians 5: 17–21

Prayer

Lord Jesus, thank You for coming to this dark, confining, terrifying world. Thank You for shining a light into my tragic and hopeless situation. Thank You for lowering Yourself to my level. Thank You for reaching out and drawing me into Your arms and saving me, though it cost Your life. Please help me overcome my fear and hesitation, surrender my comfort, and obediently and joyfully reach out to others, as You reached out to me. In Jesus' name, amen.

Simple Step: Define Your Why and What

You've already made an effort to reach out to the lost. (Notice that all five aspects of this church challenge go together). In one or two sentences, write down your understanding of why God wants you to reach out to your neighbors and friends. Then write down what you're doing or plan to do to reach out to others.

Date and initial when you complete this simple step: _____

Journal Prompt

Spend a few moments reflecting on your walk of faith. Whether you experienced new life in Christ recently or a long time ago, your present situation would have been quite different if Jesus had not reached out to you. Use the lines below to answer the question, How would my life be different if Jesus had not reached out to me?

I would not have the peace of knowing I will be with Him forever

, would not have joy in the midst of grief

May have killed myself when my depression was at its worst

Lost and Found

The famous poet, W. H. Auden, once said, "Almost all of our relationships begin and most of them continue as forms of mutual exploitation, a mental or physical barter to be terminated when one or both parties run out of goods."

In other words, most human relationships are based on some degree of selfishness. They flow from conscious or unconscious calculations: "What's in it for me?" "Will this meet my needs?" "You scratch my back, I'll scratch yours."

That's why people with a sense of humor, or a positive outlook, or a big expense account, tend to have more friends, because it's *more enjoyable* to spend time with them. That's human nature. We pursue a relationship because we get something out of it.

But Jesus said, *"The Son of Man ... came to serve, not to be served—and to give away his life"* (Mark 10:45, MSG). He doesn't seek relationships with people for what He can *get*. He seeks relationship for what He can *give*. He said, *"I came that they may have and enjoy life, and have it in abundance (to the full, till it overflows)"* (John 10:10, AMP).

Jesus said, *"Come to me, all you who are weary and burdened"* (Matthew 11:28). And He said, *"Whoever comes to me I will never drive away"* (John 6:37). And then He said this, *"Love each other as I have loved you"* (John 15:12).

Did you get that? "As I have loved you." Jesus calls us to *His* way of doing relationships, even though it is often counter-intuitive and contrary to our nature.

He calls us to seek relationships with people not for what we can *get* but for what we can *give*. Because those who are lost matter to Jesus, they should matter to us. Everyone who is missing from His sheepfold warrants an intentional, tireless search (Luke 15:3–7).

Jesus did something Jewish rabbis just didn't do. He did not wait for people to "find themselves" and then apply to follow Him as a rabbi. He sought out lost people and made them into His followers.

And Jesus had followers of all kinds. Peter with his big mouth, James and John who were always jockeying for position; Matthew, a tax collector who would have been considered a collaborator; and Mary Magdalene. She was possessed by seven demons when Jesus sought her out.

Yes, Jesus calls us to *His* way. Not our natural way, not the way our parents taught us, not the way we see other people acting around us. He calls us to *His* way.

Seeking that which is lost. Seeking relationships with people, not for what we can *get* but for what we can *give*. Lost people. Hurting people. People who may not be particularly pleasant to be around. Because Jesus' criterion for relationship was not, "What's in it for me?" It was, *"The Son of Man ... came to serve, not to be served—and to give away his life"* (Mark 10:45, MSG).

Peter, the loudmouthed, impetuous, volatile fisherman Jesus befriended one day in Galilee, ended up—of all places for a good Jew to be—not only in a Gentile's house, but in a Roman centurion's house. This is what he said to the people gathered there: *"God anointed Jesus of Nazareth with the Holy Spirit and power, and ... he went around doing good and healing all who were under the power of the devil, because God was with him"* (Acts 10:38).

"He went around doing good." And Jesus calls us to *His* way of building relationships. Seeking the lost and going around doing good because He is with us.

Scriptures

Jesus told them this parable: "Suppose one of you has a hundred sheep and loses one of them. Doesn't he leave the ninety-nine in the open country and go after the lost sheep until he finds it? And when he finds it, he joyfully puts it on his shoulders and goes home. Then he calls his friends and neighbors together and says, 'Rejoice with me; I have found my lost sheep.' I tell you that in the same way there will be more rejoicing in heaven over one sinner who repents than over ninety-nine righteous persons who do not need to repent."
—Luke 15:3–7

The Son of Man ... came to serve, not to be served—and to give away his life.
—Mark 10:45 (MSG)

Love each other as I have loved you.
—John 15:12

Prayer

Lord Jesus, thank You for seeking me and finding me when I was lost. Give me a heart for all the lost, all who are still missing from Your sheepfold. Teach me to seek relationships with people not for what I can *get* but for what I can *give*. Help me to approach all my relationships with Your heart—not to be served, but to serve, to give my life away, and to go around doing good. In Jesus' name, amen.

Simple Step: Pray for Heart

Pray the prayer above, asking that God would give you His heart for those who are lost. Make a list of people with whom you work, play, or go to school. Include those who live nearby. Everyone on that list matters to your heavenly Father. Place the list in a place where you are likely to see it every day.

Date and initial when you complete this simple step: _____

Journal Prompt

How would your relationships with people be different if you focused on what you could give and not on what you could get? How do you think that would impact your family, friends, and co-workers?

Happier

Children benifit emencly
from seeing you give

When Heaven
Throws a Party

People can find just about any reason to throw a party. Birthdays, for example. Some invite more celebration than others.

A child's first birthday is a big deal in many families. Jewish girls celebrate their bat mitzvah on their twelfth or thirteenth birthday and Jewish boys their bar mitzvah on their thirteenth birthday. Hindus practice the *Upanayana*, a "coming of age" ceremony for a twelve- or thirteen-year-old boy. Some Hispanic cultures observe a *quinceañera* celebration, marking a girl's fifteenth birthday, and many families in North America throw an elaborate "sweet sixteen" celebration for a girl's sixteenth birthday. Japan holds a Coming of Age Day for those who have turned twenty, and other Asian countries celebrate a person's sixtieth birthday.

But birthdays are only the beginning. Some of the most lavish parties are wedding celebrations. An Indian wedding lasts for days. In a Russian Orthodox wedding, the couple races each other to a special carpet where they will recite their vows. Instead of requesting "the honor of your presence," a Jewish wedding invitation invites guests to "dance at" the ceremony, which does include a lot of dancing.

Beyond birthdays and weddings, we celebrate all kinds of other occasions. We throw baby showers, welcome home parties, housewarmings, bon voyage parties, anniversary celebrations, graduation parties, office parties, costume parties, New Year's Eve bashes, Valentine's Day get-togethers, barbecues, tea parties, garden parties, and dances. The French have Bastille Day, the Swedish love their St. Lucia Festival, and the Brazilians whoop it up every year at Carnival.

It turns out that human beings are party animals. But heaven has its parties, too.

Jesus once told a series of stories about lost things. He spoke of a lost lamb that was finally found. He told of a family heirloom—a precious wedding coin—that caused a woman to turn her home upside down until she found it. He wove a tale of a wayward son who wandered far from home and family, and eventually returned.

Each of these stories ended with a lavish celebration. When the lost lamb was found, Jesus said the shepherd joyfully carried it home on his shoulders, called his friends and neighbors, and said, *"Rejoice with me; I have found my lost sheep"* (Luke 15:6). When the woman in Jesus' story located her precious coin, she called her friends and neighbors together and said, *"Rejoice with me; I have found my lost coin"* (Luke 15:9). And when the runaway returned home, the young man's father told his servants, *"Quick! Bring the best robe and put it on him. Put a ring on his finger and sandals on his feet. Bring the fattened calf and kill it. Let's have a feast and celebrate"* (Luke 15:22–23).

What can we learn from these stories?

Clearly, Jesus wants His followers to know that those who haven't yet experienced new life in Christ are inexpressibly precious to Him. Notice the metaphors Jesus chose: a lamb, an heirloom, a son. Each story reinforces the inestimable value, in God's eyes, of those who are not yet found.

Jesus wants His followers to tirelessly seek after those who haven't yet experienced new life in Christ. The shepherd goes out into the wilderness until he finds his lost sheep. The woman refuses to give up until she finds her precious coin. And, perhaps most striking of all, the prodigal's father (in a culture where it was considered undignified for a man of wealth and stature to run for any reason) threw off all restraint, *"ran to his son, threw his arms around him and kissed him"* (Luke 15:20).

Finally, Jesus wants His followers to know that reclamations bring rejoicing in heaven. That's right! Finding the lost launches parties in heaven. God and His angels applaud and celebrate whenever a lost soul comes home.

Jesus wants us to understand that we were once the lost sheep, the lost heirloom, the lost son. We bring joy to the heart of God when we turn the story around and become one who seeks that which is lost.

Scriptures

Jesus told them this parable: "Suppose one of you has a hundred sheep and loses one of them. Doesn't he leave the ninety-nine in the open country and go after the lost sheep until he finds it? And when he finds it, he joyfully puts it on his shoulders and goes home. Then he calls his friends and neighbors together and says, 'Rejoice with me; I have found my lost sheep.' I tell you that in the same way there will be more rejoicing in heaven over one sinner who repents than over ninety-nine righteous persons who do not need to repent."
—Luke 15:3–7

"Or suppose a woman has ten silver coins and loses one. Doesn't she light a lamp, sweep the house and search carefully until she finds it? And when she finds it, she calls her friends and neighbors together and says, 'Rejoice with me; I have found my lost coin.' In the same way, I tell you, there is rejoicing in the presence of the angels of God over one sinner who repents."
—Luke 15:8–10

We had to celebrate and be glad, because this brother of yours was dead and is alive again; he was lost and is found.
—Luke 15:32

Prayer

You sought me, Lord, when I was wandering far from You. Make me like You—a seeker of lost ones, a finder of precious souls, and a cause of parties in heaven. In Jesus' name, amen.

Simple Step: Make a Top Five List

From the list you made yesterday, make a "Top Five" list of skeptical or seeking people you'd like to pray for. On the left side of your paper, write their names. On the right, identify one simple step you could take to move each person closer to Christ. For one, a step might be, "Begin a friendship by _____." For another, it might be "invite them to church." And for yet another it might be "share my testimony with them."

Date and initial when you complete this simple step: _____

Journal Prompt

Choose one of the "Top Five" you listed above and describe the party heaven will throw when that person experiences new life in Christ. Use your imagination and go all out!

_____

_____

_____

_____

_____

_____

_____

_____

_____

_____

_____

Good News of Great Joy

James Marshall arrived at Sutter's Fort, an agricultural settlement in northern California, in mid-July, 1845. John Sutter, the settlement's founder, soon hired Marshall as a carpenter. A few years later, Marshall and Sutter teamed up to build a sawmill at Coloma on the American River about forty miles upstream from Sutter's Fort, east of present-day Sacramento.

On January 24, 1848, Marshall was working in the stream near the mill when he noticed some shiny flecks in the water. He picked up a couple of small chunks and turned them over in his hand. They were bright gold. He pressed a piece between two rocks and found that it could be beaten into a different shape without breaking it.

Marshall went to one of the workers, a man named Scott, and told him that he had found gold. Other members of the work crew performed additional tests, and confirmed the discovery. Marshall instructed his crew members to continue their work on the mill but allowed them to search for gold in their free time.

Before long, however, all work at the mill stopped as the men focused all their efforts on finding gold. Soon the news spread, and by the end of 1848, hordes of fortune-seekers were streaming into the area. Like the mill workers, they had abandoned everything to search for gold. By 1855, an estimated 300,000 had joined in the California Gold Rush.

Jesus once said this about the kingdom of heaven, *"The kingdom of heaven is like treasure hidden in a field. When a man found it, he hid it again, and then in his joy went and sold all he had and bought that field"* (Matthew 13:44).

In just thirty-five words (in English), Jesus depicted the kingdom of God in unmistakable terms:

- **The kingdom of heaven is a great treasure.** Jesus said the kingdom is like treasure, or as He styled it in the next breath, it is like a pearl of great price. (See Matthew 13:46.)

It is a gold mine. It is of inestimable value. The Apostle Paul spoke in similar terms (perhaps recalling Jesus' parable). He referred to *"the boundless riches of Christ … which for ages past was kept hidden in God"* (Ephesians 3:8–9).

- **Entering the kingdom of heaven is an entrance into joy.** The man in Jesus' parable went off "in his joy" to gain ownership of the treasure he had found. How often do we shrink from sharing the good news of the salvation Jesus purchased for us with others? How strange is it that we would ever hesitate for a moment to share such *"good news of great joy"* (Luke 2:10)? Have we forgotten how we came to *"believe in him and rejoice with joy that is inexpressible"* (1 Peter 1:8, esv)? Let us honor our Lord by assuming that those around us who have not yet experienced new life in Christ will be just as glad as we are to find such amazing treasure.

- **Entering the kingdom is costly, but not compared to the ultimate gain.** Jesus depicted the man in His story as selling "all he had" in order to buy the field and obtain the treasure. It is an important depiction. Matthew Henry said, "Though nothing can be given as a price for this salvation, yet much must be given up for the sake of it." We must beware of advertising a cheap gospel, while remembering Jesus' words, *"What good will it be for a man if he gains the whole world, yet forfeits his soul? Or what can a man give in exchange for his soul?"* (Matthew 16:26). Though it takes the surrender of all we have and all we are to obtain eternal life, we agree with Paul that nothing we surrender is even *"worth comparing with the glory that will be revealed in us"* (Romans 8:18).

Whatever your story is, if you are a follower of Jesus Christ, you should be enthusiastically and joyfully sharing with others, as one who has found a priceless treasure.

Scriptures

I am not ashamed of the gospel, because it is the power of God that brings salvation to everyone who believes: first to the Jew, then to the Gentile. For in the gospel the righteousness of God is revealed—a righteousness that is by faith from first to last, just as it is written: "The righteous will live by faith."
—Romans 1:16–17

"The kingdom of heaven is like treasure hidden in a field. When a man found it, he hid it again, and then in his joy went and sold all he had and bought that field.
"Again, the kingdom of heaven is like a merchant looking for fine pearls. When he found one of great value, he went away and sold everything he had and bought it."
—Matthew 13:44–46

I counsel you to buy from me gold refined in the fire, so you can become rich; and white clothes to wear, so you can cover your shameful nakedness; and salve to put on your eyes, so you can see.
—Revelation 3:18

Prayer

Gracious God, thank You for the boundless riches of Christ, which for ages past was kept hidden in God. Thank You that through faith in Him, I may approach You with freedom and confidence. Thank You for my salvation, the forgiveness of my sins, the cleansing of my heart and life, the new life I enjoy, and the eternal life I have begun. Help me to reflect such joy in my life and gratitude for my salvation that others will see and desire the priceless gift of Your salvation. In Jesus' name, amen.

Simple Step: Share Your Story

Today's journal prompt will ask you to write your story about finding new life in Christ. After you have written it, read it to at least one person (family member, friend, coworker, etc.) and ask for their feedback. That person may give you a suggestion or two for revising or refining it.

Date and initial when you complete this simple step: _____

Journal Prompt

Use the lines below to share the story of how you came to experience new life in Christ. If you're not a Christ-follower, take this opportunity to say a simple prayer asking Jesus to forgive your sins, come into your heart, and make you a new creation.

I was 10 yrs old in Bible school. Felt like I was light as a feather

Bridging the Great Divide

Ray set the tall coffee cup in front of his friend Jordan. The two of them had been having coffee for several weeks. Last week Ray had told Jordan the story of how he had become a follower of Jesus Christ, and this week he had agreed to share the good news of the gospel with him.

When they came to a comfortable break in the conversation, Ray spread out a napkin on the table in front of them and pulled out a fine-point marker. "I'm going to try to explain in a little more detail what I said last week about how I experienced new life in Jesus Christ."

Jordan nodded and sipped his coffee, so Ray drew a diagram.

"The word 'gospel' actually means 'good news,' " Ray said. "It starts with bad news, though. The figures on the left represent human beings, obviously. All of us, including you and me. On the right side, I've written God.

"As you can see, you and I are separated from God by a spiritual disease that affects us all. We all know we have this disease. It's what prevents us from reaching our potential and meeting our own standards, let alone God's standards of holiness and righteousness." He wrote the word "sin" in the center space.

"The Bible calls that disease sin, and it says that sin is what separates us from God. In the end, that separation will result in judgment and death—as well as eternal misery and regret." He wrote the words "judgment" and "death" on the left side of the figure.

Then Ray pointed with the pen to the word "God," on the right side. "But we're not the only ones with a problem. Despite our sinful condition, God loves us and wants to be in relationship with us. He wants to save us from judgment and death and give us eternal and abundant life." Ray wrote the words "eternal life" and "abundant life" on the right side of the diagram.

"So God, our heavenly Father, sent His Son Jesus to earth to be born in a miraculous way, so He would not share our spiritual disease. Jesus lived a sinless life and then became a pure and holy sacrifice for us by dying in our place. He was crucified on a wooden cross. But the story doesn't end there. On the third day, Jesus rose from the dead! He not only conquered sin but also death—for us! And He forever bridged the separation between us and God." With that, Ray drew the figure of a cross bridging the chasm in the center of his drawing and colored it in with his marker, covering the word, "sin."

"Thanks to Jesus, the way, the truth, and the life, we have access to God," Ray told Jordan. Then he pointed to the stick figures on the left side of the diagram. "It may be hard to believe, but some people actually choose to remain over there, while many, many others—myself included—have chosen life. We repented of our sin, turned our back on our old ways of living, asked God to forgive and cleanse us, invited Jesus to take up residence in our hearts, and committed to follow Jesus day by day and moment by moment. This is something we can only do with His help, of course." Ray drew an arrow from left to right, indicating the figure's movement from one side to the other.

Placing his pen on the table and pushing the napkin a few inches closer to his friend, Ray said, "So, Jordan, if you were to place yourself on this diagram, where would you be?"

Jordan tapped the left side of the diagram.

Ray nodded. "Where do you want to be?"

It took a few seconds, but finally, with the glimmer of tears in his eyes, Jordan pointed to the right side.

Ray smiled. "That's great. I can't think of any reason to wait another minute. Can you?"

Jordan smiled back, and shook his head. "No," he answered, "I don't want to wait another minute!"

To see a visual of the Bridge Illustration with similarities to the one shared in this devotional story, please go to: www.navigators.org/us/resources/illustrations/items/The%20Bridge%20to%20Life or www.themainthings.com/BridgeIllustration.htm.

Scriptures

Jesus answered, "I am the way and the truth and the life. No one comes to the Father except through me."
—John 14:6

Enter through the narrow gate. For wide is the gate and broad is the road that leads to destruction, and many enter through it. But small is the gate and narrow the road that leads to life, and only a few find it.
—Matthew 7:13–14

I am the gate; whoever enters through me will be saved. He will come in and go out, and find pasture.
—John 10:9

I am the resurrection and the life. He who believes in me will live, even though he dies.
—John 11:25

Through him we both have access to the Father by one Spirit.
—Ephesians 2:18

Prayer

Almighty God my Father, thank You for sending Jesus, born of a virgin, to be a sacrifice for my sins. Thank You for the simplicity of the gospel of my Lord Jesus Christ. Thank You that through Him I have access to You and the gift of eternal life. Thank You also for the simple tool of "The Bridge" illustration, as it was demonstrated in today's reading. Please open doors of opportunity for me to share the good news with others joyfully and enthusiastically. In Jesus' name, amen.

Simple Step: Learn the Illustration

Practice "The Bridge" illustration until you are confident you could share it with another person from memory.

Date and initial when you complete this simple step: _____

Journal Prompt

In the lines, below, write a short prayer for at least one of the people on your "Top Five" list. Ask God to prepare them as He has prepared you for a spiritual conversation in the near future.

Come and See

The gospel of Jesus Christ is a "Come and See" gospel.

When Jesus began the process of assembling His closest followers, He invited a man named Philip from the town of Bethsaida. Philip then went to his friend Nathanael and told him, "We have found the one Moses wrote about in the Torah! The one the prophets spoke of—Jesus of Nazareth, the son of Joseph." Nathanael's forehead must have wrinkled as he wondered out loud if anything good could come from a place like Nazareth.

"Come and see for yourself," said Philip. (See John 1:45–46.)

The Christian faith is an invitational faith. John the Baptist pointed to Jesus as the Anointed One. Andrew—one of John's disciples—followed Jesus. And then Andrew invited his brother, Simon Peter.

Jesus invited Philip to follow Him. And Philip, in turn, invited Nathanael with the words, "Come and see." These invitations point to some effective keys to personal outreach:

- **Earn the right to share.** Jesus could have brought forth water from a rock, but instead He opened a conversation with the Samaritan woman by asking for a drink. He had people swarming Him for healing, but He took the initiative with the man at the Pool of Bethesda. Many people see "church folk" as people who think they have all the answers. But Jesus met people where they were and started a conversation with them. We don't do that often enough. Real give-and-take relationships with the people around us will open many doors.
- **Never say no for anyone.** This principle is fundamental to the spread of the gospel in the New Testament. Jesus did not give up on the people everyone else gave up on, causing the gospel to spread rapidly because the seed was scattered everywhere. Tax collectors, Samaritans, lepers, Gentiles, and people everyone else assumed would say no to God, said yes to Jesus. So, don't underestimate the Holy Spirit's power to woo needy

hearts. You never know when a crisis will hit or a personal hurt will open a door. You never know when a heart is going to soften. So don't ever say no for anyone.

- **Extend an invitation.** Jesus said to Andrew, "Come and see." Philip said to Nathanael, "Come and see." Invite a neighbor to a special event at church. Invite a co-worker to join your small-group. Invite a friend or family member to church and then to lunch afterward. Buy an extra ticket for a concert. Offer to take someone to a special event. Invite someone to "come and see."

- **Commit to a process, not a one-time event.** Through John the Baptist, Jesus had a history with Andrew before He invited him to "come and see." Philip had probably known Nathanael for years before he said, "Come and see." If the person you invite says no, don't say, "Well, I can check that person off my list." Keep asking. It is a process.

One month, you might say, "Hey, wanna go to a cookout?" The next month, "If you're free Saturday, I've got an extra ticket to a concert I think you'll enjoy. Wanna come?" A few months later, "Hey, remember my friend you met at that concert? How about going to his house with me for a pool party?" And another time, "Remember when we talked about you feeling burned out in your job? My pastor's preaching on that Sunday. Why don't you come to church with me? I'll pick you up and we can go for coffee afterward." It's a process.

Keep your heart right. Keep the heart of Jesus toward people who seem far from God. Pray for them. Be kind and thoughtful toward them. Develop long-term relationships with them. Do everything you can to prepare for the moment when a door opens, a crack of light appears, and you have an opportunity to share the gospel in a clear and compelling way.

Scriptures

The next day John was there again with two of his disciples. When he saw Jesus passing by, he said, "Look, the Lamb of God!"
When the two disciples heard him say this, they followed Jesus. Turning around, Jesus saw them following and asked, "What do you want?"
They said, "Rabbi" (which means "Teacher"), "where are you staying?"
"Come," he replied, "and you will see."
So they went and saw where he was staying, and they spent that day with him. It was about four in the afternoon.
Andrew, Simon Peter's brother, was one of the two who heard what John had said and who had followed Jesus. The first thing Andrew did was to find his brother Simon and tell him, "We have found the Messiah" (that is, the Christ). And he brought him to Jesus.
—John 1:35–42

The next day Jesus decided to leave for Galilee. Finding Philip, he said to him, "Follow me."
Philip, like Andrew and Peter, was from the town of Bethsaida. Philip found Nathanael and told him, "We have found the one Moses wrote about in the Law, and about whom the prophets also wrote—Jesus of Nazareth, the son of Joseph."
"Nazareth! Can anything good come from there?" Nathanael asked.
"Come and see," said Philip.
—John 1:43–46

Prayer

Lord, thank You for this amazing *30-Day Church Challenge*, and for the ways it has stretched me and the lessons it has taught me. It would be a shame for me to keep all this growth and blessing to myself. I ask You for enough courage, boldness, and infectious joy to enable me to follow the example of my Lord Jesus and start conversations and build relationships that lead to eternal life. In Jesus' name, amen.

Simple Step: Do Something with Someone

Take at least one small step forward with someone on your "Top Five" list today.

Date and initial when you complete this simple step: _____

Journal Prompt

Take a few moments to look back at your journey through this *30-Day Church Challenge*. What has God done for you since then? What has He taught you? How have you changed?

How important it is to be surrounded by Gods people

In Luke 15, Jesus tells three stories. In one a shepherd has lost a sheep. In another a woman has lost a coin. The final story is about a father whose rebellious son ran away from home. In each case, something has gone missing.

In these stories, Jesus is saying, "Missing things matter enough to warrant an intentional search. Find everyone who's missing and bring them to me." We've been shown remarkable compassion. We've experienced first-hand what it's like to be lost and then found, and how it feels to be shown undeserved love, acceptance, and forgiveness. Therefore, we are compelled by the love of the Father to bring the missing to Him.

Our final challenge for this *30-Day Church Challenge* series is to care about what Jesus cares about and do something shepherd-like or woman-like or father-like to find the missing and invite them to return to God.

There are three options for your final week's challenge. You can choose one of them or all three:

- **Pray an eight-word prayer for the next eight days.** The prayer goes like this: "God, give me Your heart for the lost." It will take you just eight seconds to pray these eight words, but they are powerful. They just might change your life.
- **Invite a friend to church.** You can simply say, "I've been going to (name of church) and really enjoying it. Would you like to come with me this Sunday?"
- **Share your faith with someone.** In this week's readings, you came across a simple method for explaining the gospel called "The Bridge." Your challenge, should you choose to accept this option, is to share your faith with someone.

Small-Group Study
and Discussion Questions

For use by small-groups after the Week 5 readings on the topic of Outreach.

Below is a complete list of small-group study and discussion questions that will cover some of the important themes for this week. We have also included questions regarding the videos that your small-group will watch. In order to stay within the time limits of your small-group meeting, your small-group leader will choose what questions he or she wants your group to focus on. You will need to bring your book with you to your small-group or class.

1. Open in prayer.
2. **Video Stories.** What insights did you gain from watching the video stories by Brae and Kevin? How did God speak to you through their testimonies?
3. **Video Stories.** After becoming a Christian, Kevin invited his family to church, and they became Christians. Who is God putting on your heart to invite to church? when?
4. **Video Stories.** Brae shared how God used his son's youth pastor to deliver His personal message so that Brae could come to Christ. After his salvation, Brae became God's instrument to deliver His personal message to others. Who did God use to deliver His personal message to you? How have you been used by God to deliver His personal message to family, friends, or others?
5. Go around the room asking everyone to briefly describe the following: Describe a time when you got lost or needed directions.
6. Read Luke 15:1–7 together.
7. Who is in Jesus' audience as He tells this parable? How do they respond to Him?
8. How does Jesus' parable of the sheep relate to the Pharisees? How does it relate to the tax collectors and sinners with whom Jesus was eating?

(Questions continued on the next page.)

9. What was the main point of Jesus' story?
   ___Most people don't need to repent.
   ___The Pharisees were righteous.
   ___Finding lost sheep is heaven's top priority.
   ___Don't look down on tax collectors and sinners.
   ___Other
10. With whom do you most identify in this story? Jesus? the tax collectors and sinners? the Pharisees? the lost sheep? the ninety-nine sheep? why?
11. How does this story affect your attitude toward God?
12. How do you think this story should affect your attitude toward other people?
13. What do you think would be an appropriate response to this story for us as a group?
14. What do you think would be an appropriate response to this story for you as an individual?
15. How do you react to this statement, from the Day 27 reading in the *30-Day Church Challenge* book: "We who were once the lost sheep … bring joy to the heart of God when we turn the story around and become one who seeks that which is lost"?
16. What, if anything, is keeping you from more actively reaching out to those who haven't yet found their way to the Savior?
17. Name one way you as an individual, or together with the other members of this group, can more actively reach out to those who haven't yet experienced new life in Christ.
18. Any other questions or comments?
19. Take a few moments in a closing period of prayer, and pray especially for any "lost sheep" around you.

INSIDE THE STORIES: VIDEO TESTIMONY BIOGRAPHIES

The following are short biographies from each contributor who shared their video story in the DVD portion of the 30-Day Church Challenge DVD-based Study Kit, of which this book is a part.

WEEK ONE: COMMUNITY

Quay Ball *is a mother and stepmother of six beautiful children and lives in Carlsbad, California, with her husband, Chip. She has a BA in elementary education from Anderson University and has taught Kindergarten and 2nd Grade. As a trauma survivor; Quay uses her past to help women experience healing through intimacy with Jesus. She is a trainer and speaker with Healed Heart Encounter and is involved in many different ministries including: Women's Bible Study Teacher, Prayer Counselor and Worship and Prayer Leader.*

Ailina Carona *and her husband, Rob, are leaders at their church's college and career group, as well as the worship team. She is passionately and purposefully in pursuit of an intimate relationship with Jesus. Ailina looks forward to one day traveling with her husband around the world and helping people encounter the love and goodness of Jesus.*

Justin Haag *lives in Oceanside, CA. He works in the youth ministry and is currently pursuing a career in Criminal Justice. Justin wants to become a U.S. Marshall and help put an end to human trafficking.*

WEEK TWO: WORSHIP

Rob Carona *and his wife, Ailina, are involved as leaders at their church's college and career group, as well as the worship team. He's a songwriter and loves playing music (you can check out his music at www.youtube.com/thecaronas music). Rob also loves sports, being outdoors, and most of all ... sharing the love of Jesus!*

Adam *is the evangelism and outreach pastor at a church in Southern California. He is happily married to a wonderful woman named Cleta. And God has graciously blessed them both with their daughter, Bella. He is a living example of what great things God can do! One of his favorite verses from the Bible is: "For I am not ashamed of the gospel, because it is the power of God that brings salvation to everyone who believes ..." (Romans 1:16).*

WEEK THREE: SPIRITUAL GROWTH

Julia Mottola *is a stay-at-home mom. She is married with two teenage daughters, Sierra and Frankie. Julia accepted Christ as her Savior in 2005 and attends New Song Community Church in Oceanside, CA. She now serves the Lord as the director of a ministry called Trash to Treasure Recycling Ministry. The ministry supports eighty-five war orphans in Liberia and a local group called Solutions for Change for homeless families, all through recycling. The website is www.recyclingministry.com.*

Cyrus Greene *is a licensed pastor and ordained minister who helps run Next Door Ministries and the food pantry. He also preaches at the homeless shelter and is on staff at his church, being responsible for managing the facilities. He is involved in the Bread of Life, Celebrate Recovery, Brothers and Sisters in Christ, and Brother Benno's ministries. Cyrus lives in Oceanside, CA.*

WEEK FOUR: STEWARDSHIP

Jim Britts *is the next generation pastor at New Song Community Church in Oceanside, CA. where he's been on staff since 2002. He has a smoking hot wife (Rachel) and the cutest kid in the world (Jadon). He is a die hard Sacramento Kings fan, a professional in Costco sampling, and he loves to run for fun. He also wrote the script to the movie* To Save a Life *and he has authored a couple of books with* *his wife. Jim loves pouring into teenagers and helping them figure out how God wants to use them to change their world.*

Jennifer Kay *is an inspirational speaker and author who uses the trials she faced as a testimony to others that even in the midst of impossibilities, all things really are possible through the strength of God. She longs to help others who have been caught in the web of drugs, addictions, and turmoil find the strength in Jesus to turn their lives around. Jennifer is a featured author in the best-selling book,* Bouncing Back: Thriving in Changing Times. *Her website is, www. WheelOfftheWagon.com.*

WEEK FIVE: OUTREACH

Brae Wyckoff, *born and raised in San Diego, CA, has been married to his beautiful wife, Jill, for eighteen years. They have three children: Tommy, Michelle, and Brittany. He and his wife are the founders of The Greater News Facebook page: www.facebook.com/thegreaternews, which reports on miracles, signs, and wonders from around the world. Brae is the author of* The Orb of Truth, *the first in a series of fantasy action adventures laced with Christian undertones: www. theorboftruth.com. Brae co-hosts a radio program called* Prophetic Underground, *which can be found at www.propheticunderground.com, Facebook, and iTunes.*

Kevin Conway *lives in Vista, CA where he is busy raising his fifteen-year-old son and eighteen-year-old niece. Kevin is actively involved in church and serves as an usher, greeter, and small-group leader. In his free time he likes to bodysurf, snowboard, and ride mountain bikes.*

ARE YOU READY TO TAKE THE CHALLENGE?

The *30-Day Church Challenge DVD-Based Study* is a five-week study based on the foundational Scriptures regarding the early Church in the book of Acts, and is specifically designed to help you or your small-group discover and learn how to reach your God-given potential through the five purposes of the church.

Participants will be encouraged to develop a stronger relationship with God, engage their lives in priorities that really matter, connect deeper with others, and reach out to friends, family, and acquaintances with God's love. The kit includes everything you need for individual or group study, including a DVD with video stories and testimonies for each week, a *Leader's Guide* (for use in small-group setting), and the *30-Day Church Challenge* book with daily devotional lessons, a personal journaling section, and small-group or individual study and discussion questions.

The 30-Day Church Challenge DVD-Based Study Kit is available online or at your local Christian bookstore. Bulk quantities available at Outreach, Inc.

THIRTY DAYS THAT WILL TRANSFORM YOUR CHURCH!

For many, unfortunately, the church is only a place they go to on Sundays or holidays. **What if it could be much more?** The *30-Day Church Challenge* is a five-week campaign based on the foundational Scriptures in the book of Acts and is specifically designed to help every church attender engage in the five purposes of the church, and be challenged to reach their God-given potential. Featuring inspirational sermons, resource DVD with sermon illustrations, weekly challenges, church leader's guide, planning and idea guide, DVD-based study for small-groups, PowerPoint templates and matching bulletin inserts, and planning and promotional tools! At the end of the *30-Day Church Challenge* your congregation won't just come to church, they will **Become** the church: A community of faith—powerful, inspirational, and transformational—touching your community and the world with the power of the gospel!

The 30-Day Church Challenge Church Kit is available online or at your local Christian bookstore. Bulk quantities available at Outreach, Inc.

TAKE YOUR GROUP
OR YOURSELF ON A GODQUEST!

GodQuest is a six-week study that answers the most critical challenges facing you on your spiritual journey! No matter where you are in your spiritual life, this easy-to-use study can guide you and your group into a stronger, deeper relationship with the one, true God. *GodQuest* presents six signposts with powerful truths and compelling evidence on the topics of God, creation, the Bible, Jesus, pain and suffering, and the path to heaven. The twelve- to seventeen-minute video lessons include teaching by dynamic speaker Sean McDowell, guest appearances by leading scholars, inspiring personal testimonies, historic sites in Israel, and dramatic scientific evidence.

The GodQuest DVD-Based Study Kit is available online or at your local Christian bookstore. Bulk quantities available at Outreach, Inc.